GOD'S GIFT

THE LOVE OF A MOTHER
(WHY DO YOU HATE ME SO MUCH)

Why Do You Hate Me
Copyright © Katrina Casandra Newman 2018 All Rights Reserved
The rights of Katrina Casandra Newman to be identified as the author of this work have been asserted in accordance with the Copyright, Designs and Patents Act 1988
All rights reserved. No part may be reproduced, adapted, stored in a retrieval system or transmitted by any means, electronic, mechanical, photocopying, or otherwise without the prior written permission of the author or publisher.
Spiderwize
Remus House
Coltsfoot Drive
Woodston
Peterborough
PE2 9BF
www.spiderwize.com
A CIP catalogue record for this book is available from the British Library.
The views expressed in this work are solely those of the author and do not necessarily reflect the views of the publisher, and the publisher hereby disclaims any responsibility for them.
ISBN: 978-1-912694-66-2

THE LOVE OF A MOTHER

WHY DO YOU HATE ME SO MUCH?

KATRINA CASANDRA NEWMAN

SPIDERWIZE
Peterborough UK
2018

Contents

FOREWORD 1
INTRODUCTION 2
CHAPTER 1 MY FAMILY 5
CHAPTER 2 THE DAY MY LIFE CHANGED FOREVER 15
CHAPTER 3 THE HYDE JUNIOR SCHOOL 17
CHAPTER 4 HIGH SCHOOL 20
CHAPTER 5 MY LIFE WAS IN DANGER 24
CHAPTER 6 FIGHT LIKE A MAN 30
CHAPTER 7 MOTHER WHY CAN'T YOU HEAR ME? 33
CHAPTER 8 THE PARTY LIFE 36
CHAPTER 9 SWEET SIXTEEN 41
CHAPTER 10 WATFORD: THE YMCA 43
CHAPTER 11 WHY DO YOU HATE ME SO MUCH? 81
CHAPTER 12 BEAUTIFUL PAIN 98
CHAPTER 13 DO YOU BELIEVE IN MARRIAGE? 99
CHAPTER 14 THE DAY I NEARLY DIED 120
CHAPTER 15 FRIENDSHIP 146
CHAPTER 16 WHAT ARE YOU RUNNING FROM? 147
CHAPTER 17 WHO AM I ? KATRINA CASSANDRA NEWMAN ... 148
CHAPTER 19 DEPRESSION 155

CHAPTER 20 PERFECT LOVE 157

CHAPTER 21 MY FATHER 158

CHAPTER 22 I NEEDED YOU 160

CHAPTER 23 I CRY 162

CHAPTER 24 SANDRA NEWMAN 163

CHAPTER 25 FORGIVING LOVE 168

CHAPTER 26 POURING OUT MY LOVE LETTER 175

CHAPTER 27 THE OLD DEAL 177

CHAPTER 28 THE FUTURE AND GIVING BACK 178

ACKNOWLEDGEMENTS 182

ABOUT THE AUTHOR 184

I dedicate this book to the (Old Me) thank you for the life experiences, the learning curve, the honesty, the heartbreak and the sharpness. Thank you so so much for that tough ride, it was a pleasure. We got through the roughness. It can only get better. Here's to the future!

Love from the New Katrina

When you sell yourself the Dream

When you dream a dream so big you believe nothing can stop you. The previous me had great ideas for my future, it was overly loved with happiness. When I was a young girl my eagerness was simple, all I wanted was to be married own a four-bedroom house in Hertfordshire with my puppy Rottweiler named star. Five kids: three boys and two girls. Their names would be Sunnie, Boobie, Loui, Kayleigh-Jade, and Jodie-Lee. A car that was working fine, my husband would have a good job running his own business. I'd become an actress and write my own movies. I loved that feeling believing my name would be sparkling all over the globe for everyone to see. I quickly learned that life can change in a heartbeat if you don't continue to believe in yourself and your dreams. People only hear what they want you to become. I still dream that one day I will have that big four bedroom house in Hertfordshire with my perfect husband and five kids. I'm ready to grab the blessings I have been missing out on. 2019 is the year and I'm making sure of that it is finally time to become me.

Words only become powerful if you start to believe them, when they become what we think of ourselves.

I've come to the understanding that how people treat you, whether it is good or bad, is a choice that they choose for themselves.

FOREWORD

Katrina writes a honest and challenging autobiography which centres around the desire for the love of a mother in her life. Through a literary emotional rollercoaster, we are guided through her young life growing up on the West Hendon Estate in NW London from school to motherhood, and how through all the difficult times, God was with her protecting her from sometimes certain death.

As one reads through Katrina's story, we also join her on her personal spiritual journey, as she outgrows the old Katrina to blossom into the new Katrina who is reborn in Christ. At the end of her journey, she no longer craves for the love of her mother, as she is now filled with God's love which has been poured into her heart through the Holy Spirit (cf. Rom. 5:5). In fact, as we follow her story, we discover that Katrina now becomes the source of a mother's love not only to her daughter Kayleigh, but to others that she shares the message of Jesus with.

This book is a testimony of the providence of God in Katrina's life. What the devil meant for evil against her, God has turned around for her own good and his own glory; in order to bring to faith many people, through the testimony of his daughter Katrina Cassandra Newman (cf. Gen. 50:20; Rom. 8:28).

I trust that as you read this book that not only will you receive some good wise insights into the importance of knowing yourself in order not to be manipulated by others, but also learn about the grace of God that will see you through the inevitable difficult times that you will encounter in life.

Grace & Peace.

Winston Bygrave

Minister of West Hendon Baptist Church, London.

INTRODUCTION

Only God himself can justify the wrongdoings of men and women. I just don't understand how you can hurt the one thing God gave to you as a gift; a life to bring forth into the world to nurture, love and grow. I will never understand it. I have learned to forgive but I will never forget the pain and suffering I endured throughout my years growing up. The learning experience was not a good one but I made a good experience come out of it. It has taught me to be strong, independent and caring, but most of all it has taught me how to love myself and love others. It has made me the person I am today.

I'm sitting here wondering how the hell am I going to execute this book? How do I start to write about my life journey? I'm a very private person and I do not like people in my business so for me to talk about my life story and my personal affairs publicly is going to be very challenging for me.

I'm not much of a writer but I love telling stories. The hardest part about this story is that it's my own life story. I'm scared, excited and anxious. I wear my heart on my sleeve; what you see is what you get with me, so when telling my story I'm going to be as honest as I can be. No shortcuts, no corners missed. I've put my laptop down more than enough times thinking why am I doing this? What can this achieve? If my story makes one person think in regards to their actions and what damage it can cause to a person's well-being then I've done my job.

I have wasted enough time on people and left my life behind. Forgiveness is a form of love, but don't be stupid with it, don't forget how people have treated you: that is their real character and some things are unforgettable. The impact people can leave behind after the damage they have done makes you think how on earth can you forgive someone so heartless?

Some people are so blinded by their pain they forget to see the beauty within themselves. Forgive them and guide them: holding on to painful memories will rob you of your happiness and joy. You're stuck because you won't make a change. You're stuck because you won't let go. Take the pain away and turn your sad memories into happy memories and set yourself free.

My mother has always claimed she has mental health problems and a part of me believes her for her bizarre behaviour; how can you be fine one minute and then switch within a split second for no reason at all? Is it a sympathy vote my mother is looking for? Is she a bully? Is it the drugs she takes? Is it the alcohol she drinks? What is it? To be honest I don't want to stick around to find out what my mother is thinking or why she behaves the way she does; I have a life to live and I'm finally going to live it.

I know this is not going to be an easy read for my mother, but it's my life story. It's not about my mother, it's about me. My mother is a part of my life journey my story is not based on her, it's based on the impact my life has had on me, my life struggles and my upbringing which has contributed to my life mistakes and positive achievements and finding myself along the way.

My name is Katrina Cassandra Newman. I was born and raised in London, England. I was born in Edgware Hospital in 1983 to parents Sandra Newman and Ronald Thomas. I come from the typical black family: absent father, child raised by mother. It's sad to say but about 60% of black families are missing black fathers*.

I have an older brother called Leonardo (we share a father but have different mothers) and a younger brother called Ben. Being the only girl, both of my brothers do my head in and I'm always telling both my brothers off, but boys will be boys.

I have a daughter called Kayleigh-Jade Jah Princess Felix. Kayleigh was born at the Royal Free Hospital on 9th April 2012. Kayleigh is a big blessing in my life and I adore her very much, I appreciate this cheeky munchkin I really do.

Before Kayleigh was even thought about I suffered two miscarriages. The second one I had was so severe I ended up getting an infection in the middle of my inner ear which has caused me to have balance and vision problems which made me very unwell. Mentally, emotionally

*www.runnymedetrust.org

and physically this drained my soul. I can never explain the pain and suffering I have been through. I would never wish this on my worst enemy and believe me I have many enemies. It didn't help that I did not get any support on how to deal with such a loss. All I was ever taught in life was "Get over it, you're not the only one going through this." Mothers aye, aren't they loving!

I know it sounds harsh but this became my reality, a normal way of life, a normal way of living, a normal way of thinking.

I adapted to being heartless, something you can master when you've never been shown how to love.

This is why I cherish my baby girl so much; she is a blessing from God. She is so special and it's a love that is out of my control, a love that's unconditional.

I'm writing my autobiography at the age of thirty-four because I feel this is the right time for me to do this. Everything in life has its timing and everything happens for a reason. I want people to hear my story: maybe some people can relate to it, maybe some people might understand it, but the main reason why I'm writing this book is for me. I have a story to tell from my heart. Throughout my life I never had a voice; people always dictated my life for me. I have a voice now and it needs to be heard. My story has many negatives but it also has many positives. I want to show the world that no matter what you go through in life, no matter how hard it gets, you can always turn a negative situation into a positive. I'm living proof of this.

I'm starting my new journey, my new chapter and I look forward to the new beginnings ahead. I can finally see what life is all about. I'm happy, I'm blessed: what more could I ask for out of life? I'm grateful for the lessons and I'm grateful for the blessing.

You are made up of a lot of things from your life, it's true, and appearances can hide a lot of secrets.

The lack of upbringing, the lack of love, being completely forgotten about, the pain and torment can turn you into a troubled soul.

This is my story.

CHAPTER 1
MY FAMILY

My grandparents Alwyn Newman and Clarice Newman are from the West Indies.

They were invited to come over to England in the 1950s from the Caribbean island of St Kitts. My grandmother had a son prior to meeting my grandfather called Alfred. She left him in St Kitts while they came with their two children, Pearl and Sylreeta aged five and six. They settled in Cricklewood, North West London.

My grandfather was of mixed heritage. I recently found out his father was a white Scotsman and my great grandfather's mother was Chinese. I knew my grandfather was mixed race as he looked more Asian but I thought it was Indian, now I know he has Chinese heritage.

I'm not going to lie, hearing about my grandfather's history for the first time I was kind of pissed off. I had been claiming for years Indian was my duel heritage along with Caribbean. It upset me but hey it is what it is, you can't deny your DNA! I see where my family gets the fiery side.

Soon after they settled in London the other siblings followed: John, Stephen, Anthony, Shirley, Sandra and Keith. The family of four became the family of ten.

The regeneration was happening in West Hendon and my grandparents were offered a four-bedroom house, which is still the family home to this present day.

My family tells me many stories of good times and bad times at the family home and I love hearing them. The one thing I love hearing about is how much they all got along with their neighbours and how much they were a community. Even in those racist times in the early 60s they all came together.

My grandfather was such a sharp dresser. I would catch him along West Hendon Broadway after he had a few drinks inside him, dressed in his best immaculate suit, singing out loud with a broom or doing some kind of funky dance or trying the MJ. When he would see me coming up the Broadway he would always dance with me and give me and a girl I grew up with, Natasha, some sweets from the stale liquor store Charlie's on West Hendon Broadway. The shop's gone now due to the regeneration happening in the area. The sweets were so old you would have to blow dust from the container to see what sweets you were buying and they had a dam cheek when you stole a sweet to get angry. Natasha and I would steal sweets from Charlie's regularly. They wouldn't complain because my granddad would do little errands for them and they knew the sweets were full of shit and no good to eat. What a legend my grandfather was. I miss him dearly and my grandmother too. If I could have one minute with them I would pour my love all over them.

I grew up on the West Hendon council estate at the back of the Welsh Harp River. It was one of the nicest council estates you would have ever seen in your life, full of greenery, full of nature. This is why I loved my area; I was free to run around without a care in the world.

I lived with my grandmother, granddad, mother, uncles Anthony and Keith and cousin Leroy. The other family members upped and left the family home.

My mother Sandra had me at the age of sixteen. There are no pictures of my mother and me together when I was younger, I'm guessing she was young and was camera shy but there are many pictures of me with other family members, friends and associates.

Living with such a large family had hard times. My grandfather and Uncle John became alcoholics and the house was dysfunctional. I don't remember much but I do remember my mother arguing with her dad and brother John, seeing her crying and screaming down the house. The arguments became normal to me. I was never scared, I think I was programmed that this was how family life was supposed to be. It became the normality of my surroundings.

With all the madness going on I still had great times. I was raised by my grandparents and uncles. My mother was there but she wasn't there; she was partying, living her life, being free. She had me young so I guess she still had a young attitude.

Thank God for my family, I loved living with them and I got away with murder. Before my uncle Anthony moved out of the family home he would take me and my cousin Syreeta on trips everywhere: day trips to McDonald's, holidays to Devon, midnight feasts, midnight drives up to London. We even recorded a song with him. "Puurapartyyyy ah purrteta pura." Singing that song at this present time while I'm writing my book brings back so many happy memories. If I had one chance to go back into my childhood I would, even for a split second just to feel those memories again. I was well looked after.

We can say we were very lucky to have family looking out for us. Growing up I was very close to my uncle Anthony and uncle Keith. My uncle Keith taught me how to play football. I mastered the craft of football and was the best in my area, better than some boys and at such a young age I could run fast with the ball, tackle the opposition, dive and score some banging goal.

My uncle Keith got me to support Liverpool FC. I'd sit with him in the back bedroom watching Liverpool FC play and he would tell me, "Katrina that's me there on the pitch." I'd stare at the TV thinking John Barnes was my uncle Keith on the TV.

Keith was so good at football and he resembles John Barnes so much I couldn't tell if it was him or not.

Everyone around the West Hendon area knows my uncle Keith from old to young and it's all about football. They always come running up to me saying, "Your uncle oh my god, your uncle Keith what a great footballer." He could have been one of the best. Keith was so good at football he would teach all the kids at the back of our house on the fields including myself and they would call him John Barnes, a legend in the making.

Uncle Keith told me a story, he could have become a professional football player but my grandmother would not sign the papers for him to play professional for Barnet FC. I'm guessing my grandmother thought that it was not a career for a young black male in racist England in the 1970s. She might have thought he wouldn't make it far being a footballer. My nan was very old-school and she would have thought Keith playing football would not get him anywhere in life. How sad, football is my uncle Keith's life and passion, you can clearly see that he loves football. Sleeps, eats, shits football: yep that's my uncle Keith. We talk in depth now and I feel really sad for him because he didn't get to fulfill his dream of becoming a great footballer. Keith is one of the good guys, one of the good fellas. A man I will forever cherish.

My cousins Syreeta, Earl and Emma would often pass over or stay in the summer holidays. Emma lived in Wiltshire, we never got to see Emma much but when we did it was nice to see her. As I lived with my grandparents they would visit me there. My younger cousins Sophia, Aaron, Amari Syan and Freddie Lee came on the scene later. I know for sure they would have got the same treatment I got and been well loved if my grandparents were still alive.

Syreeta was the only cousin who was down most of the time as she lived not too far from the family home. My auntie Shirley would come to see her mum and dad and visit the family. Syreeta was the only cousin I grew up close to. In the family home where you see me you would see Syreeta.

Apparently as I have been told I was a little rebel to my cousin Syreeta. How, I don't know as she is three years older than me, but she was quiet and I was boisterous and full of energy. One time me and Syreeta were eating our breakfast in the kitchen on the breakfast table. My grandmother had made us cereal and Syreeta and me were eating. When my grandmother turned away I spat in Syreeta's breakfast, then carried on eating mine. Syreeta was crying but my grandmother didn't want to hear her story. "Eat up your damn breakfast," my grandmother said sternly to Syreeta as her eyes filled with tears. She was forced to eat her breakfast with my saliva running all through it. I actually don't remember this incident but I often get reminded by my cousin Syreeta of the events that occurred in the family home.

Most of my time was spent at the family home. Growing up was full of enjoyment and happy times. Syreeta and me used to play a game, Judie and Sarah's, where we role-played a scene and used the washing machine as if we were going on a journey up to London. How we had such an imagination at such a young age is kind of interesting, the kids of today won't understand that. We had great times bouncing off each other and being close to the same age really helped. I think there were a few incidents between me and Syreeta and I was the one instigating it or causing it but I actually don't remember them. I'm glad I don't remember. I can't stand bullies and to think I was bullying my older cousin is awful.

Syreeta told me of an incident when I pulled a knife on her and put it up against her neck with the words, "If you fucking tell anyone I will kill you."

I must have been about eight years of age. Even hearing that I did such a manic act really scared me and to do that at that age, what had I been exposed to? I asked Syreeta, "Are you sure I did that?" It made me feel sick to my stomach hearing it, how could I be so violent at such a young age?

Syreeta was a quiet child and I was rebellious, bold and confident. It's like life has taken a turn because now Syreeta is loud and bold, and I'm shy, cool, calm and collected. You see, never underestimate how life can turn out. Life can be really crazy. Now you can't shut Syreeta up!

I moved out of the family home when my grandparents passed away. My grandmother passed away when I was ten years of age. She became unwell after falling and hurting her back taking me to school. I blamed myself for her death for many years and wrote a letter to my uncle Anthony saying I wanted to take myself out of this world. I thought I had hurt my grandmother. I felt that if she'd never taken me to school she never would have fallen and she would still be alive. I couldn't understand how she was fit and well one minute and then in a hospital bed paralysed from the neck down. I was gutted. This was my worst nightmare: my main rock was gone and I felt alone.

My grandmother would do everything for the family, especially me. I was the only grandchild that lived in the family home and I had an amazing bond with my family and my grandparents. My grandmother was the queen bee, she kept me healthy, kept me clean, a proper cooked meal: no fast food, no KFC, no euro fried chicken, proper cooked food from scratch. My grandmother would give Syreeta and me cod liver oil washed down with Vimto every Saturday morning to cleanse us. I hated it but I appreciate it now. My grandmother was looking after me. I thought it was torture but she was making my bones strong, my body strong, Thank you Nan.

My grandmother would never say I love you, but I knew deep down in her heart she loved me dearly and she would show this to me by the way she looked after me.

My grandmother would hold me, hug me and kiss me; I was always in her arms. I would sit on her lap and chat to her for hours. How she was so content I do not know. There can never be a price on the love my grandmother showed me and gave me. I have never felt that love again. No amount of money in this world could ever compare to my grandmother's love. I was rich in love. Even though my life ended up miserable I was so happy with my family and grandparents. If my grandparents were alive today they would be well looked after. My grandmother gave me things I can never repay her for: a roof over my head, love and patience and I'm ever so grateful for this. I was always smartly dressed and well groomed, I was never fancy or designer dressed but my clothes were good. My grandmother used to buy my clothes from Burnt Oak market and the shoe shop on the Broadway. Getting my feet measured was like a day trip and that was across the road. I was never taken anywhere abroad on holiday, but I would go to the seaside for the day. That's classed as a day holiday and that's what I went on. I enjoyed it very much running around the beach. I have some of the best memories from those days.

I never really spent time with my mother, I was always shoved somewhere else. My mother never took me anywhere with just us two alone, there was always someone around in our home or if we were going out and on day trips there would be a load of us going up to the seaside and I always spent my time with other people, at other people's houses or was sent somewhere. It was okay for my mother to have a life but she could have spent some time with me. I actually don't remember a time I spent with my mother as a young child just me and her. Nope, there's none. She never spent any quality time with me, not even to lunch. There was no mother-daughter bonding. I was her only child at that time; you would think a mother would give their love to their only child. While all other families and my cousins were travelling the world and having family functions and family time I was just there floating about, enjoying my little childhood day-to-day.

KATRINA CASANDRA NEWMAN

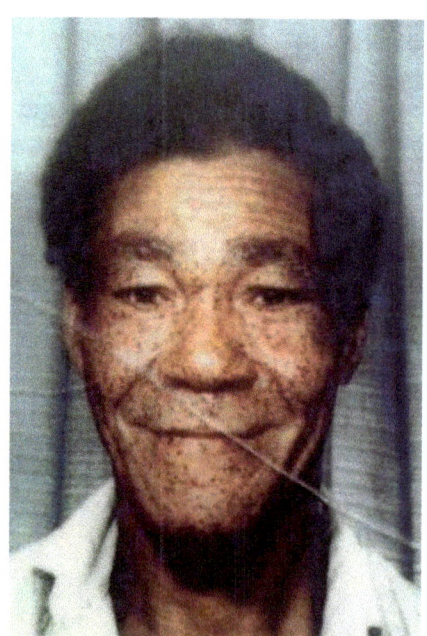

My grandparents Clarice Newman and
Alwyn Newman from St Kitts Nevis West Indies

THE LOVE OF A MOTHER

My uncle John's wedding with family members and me as a bridesmaid

Me and my main man uncle Keith

Me and my grandmother Clarice Newman

CHAPTER 2
THE DAY MY LIFE CHANGED FOREVER

I remember it like yesterday. I was sitting in my mother's living room when my mother told me and my cousin Syreeta and auntie Shirley our grandmother had passed away. I was devastated. The day before we had just seen my grandmother in hospital, she was talking and she seemed okay. My grandmother was my world, my peace, my love and I had lost my main support. I was lost, what was I going to do? My grandmother passed away in Edgware Hospital in 1994 at the tender age of sixty-six. Three months later my grandfather passed away from a broken heart at the age of seventy. As I watched my world crumble around me, nothing could prepare me for what was in store for my future ahead. My grandmother had always protected me, nurtured and guided me. Who was going to take care of me now?

After both my grandparents passed away I officially moved in with my mother. My uncle Keith still resided at the family address along with my cousin Leroy. My uncle Anthony was soon to be married and was getting ready to leave the family home.

My mother was now my main carer. It wasn't going to be easy for her, she was now having to look after me twenty-four seven which I think my mother found hard to do. Her mother had done everything for her children, even as grown adults, especially my mother. She was free to do as she pleased and even though my uncles and aunties were around they started to live their own lives. It was different for me, I spent all my time in the family home and now I would only pass through to visit. No Nanny, no Granddad. I didn't have any grief counselling. Come to think of it I just got on and played with my friends. I do remember a time I went to school and everyone was being nice to me. I didn't realise that they knew my grandmother had passed away so they were being sensitive towards me, which was nice but it soon went back to the same old playing in school.

After a few months I left my feelings of sorrow and got on with school. There was no more talk of my grandparents. That was it, they were gone and I had to get on with life.

CHAPTER 3
THE HYDE JUNIOR SCHOOL

The primary school I attended was called The Hyde Junior School based in North West London, a five minute walk from where I lived on the West Hendon estate. Everyone from my area went to that school and we all grew up together. There were many different cultures and races: white, black, Asian, but we never saw each other's colour, we just saw each other as friends. We all got along uniting together. We made a community; we played and had the best fun. Our parents either went to school with one another or knew each other from around the estate. You can say the community was tight-knit, everyone knew each other and we all had one special thing in common: we came from that estate in West Hendon.

Before the Hyde School, I went to the local nursery in West Hendon with the local kids. I attended the nursery until I was three then I moved to the Hyde School Nursery. Mona, who is my mum's good friend, was the manager at the nursery. I was well looked after. My memory is vague in regards to the nursery in the West Hendon estate but I get mini flashbacks of playing in the nursery garden with my friends. I can picture my little self running around the playground. That's one of my happy memories; it makes me smile a lot when I think of how free I used to be.

The nursery was knocked down and houses have been placed there. When I walk past my old nursery and see the houses I stand and stare and wonder what has happened to the other children at the nursery, where could they be, what has their life mapped out to be? I wonder if they think the same. I think about many facts of my life, unequal parts. I wonder and worry a lot; why I think this way only God knows.

At the Hyde Junior School I went on many school trips and I was the only girl allowed to play on the boy's football team because I was great at football. The skills taught to me by my uncle Keith never left my feet. I did enjoy those times always playing football or playing out.

I was picked for the school's play Joseph and the Amazing Technicolor Dreamcoat. I had a small part in that which also built up my confidence. I used to be very shy but when I was acting, singing, or playing football it brought out the best in me and when I wasn't doing this I was feeling lost and didn't know my position in life. That's how I knew this was my passion and I really wanted to pursue this dream.

Primary school was a laugh and fun times, some of the best years growing up.

Outside of school in my personal life I was occupied. I attended drama school, played football and came close to winning a pageant. I wouldn't speak at the pageant (now you can't shut me up) and the judges were telling my mother, "Please let her just say her name and she will win she's so cute." But nope I wasn't having any of it, not a single word out of my mouth. Everyone was pissed, even the judges, so I came second. The judges really wanted me to win. When me and my mother went for some lunch afterwards the judges were still on my case because they really wanted me to win, but I was just a kid and all I wanted was to go out and play. I was in the local paper riding on a float with all the contestants riding around the local town in Barnet showing off our crowns and waving our wands. That was a nice experience.

I went to a drama school in Mill Hill. I can't remember the name of the drama school I attended but I remember you had to audition to get in and I passed every audition with flying colours and hardly spoke. I was able to read the lines and act out the scene so naturally where the other kids forced it. I don't know what people could see in me but they saw potential in me somewhere. I had an audition for Pride and Prejudice and got the part but my mother didn't pay the fees for the next term. I remember begging my mother but she didn't budge. Who knows why she didn't pay the fees but all I know is that I was pissed for years because this was what I loved. I was so good at acting and would have been one the great actresses of all time. I can proudly boast this because I know I could act; it was where I found peace.

Those are some of my proudest moments, memories I cannot forget. They mean so much to me. I do sit down and think what could have been but that just fucks up my head even more, so I take it as a lovely memory and leave it at that. When I stopped going to drama school I gave up on everything. There was nothing that could keep me happy and focused so I rebelled.

CHAPTER 4
HIGH SCHOOL

I had a lot of good times with my family after my grandparents passed away but no guidance; I was left to do what I wanted. Now I think of it my family unit was fading away and everyone was just living their own life, all of them grieving for the one person who kept the family together: my grandmother.

After leaving the Hyde School I was forced to go to Hendon School. I remember getting the news, I was so upset because all my friends were going to Edgware High School. There was no one I knew at Hendon and I would have to make new friends. My mother wanted to keep on the tradition; she went to Hendon School and so should I. I was never allowed to have a say in anything so I had to go to Hendon School. I ended up leaving after rebelling and ended up going to the school of my choice, Edgware. I was so happy.

The first person to introduce me to smoking was a girl I grew up with. The cigarette would drop from the top balcony and she would pick the cigarette butt up off the floor and try to smoke it. Like a fool I would follow suit as she would egg me on to take a toke. We would have been eight or nine years old. Alcohol was also introduced to me and how to steal a car was also taught to me, but people always make assumptions that I was the sneaky one. Sometimes it's best to sit back and not say a word, but observe the situation and make your own assumptions.

Smoking and drinking became a normal part of my life and I started to like it a few years later.

I was exposed to sexual activities at young age by a relative. It didn't feel right what was happening to me but being so young and not being taught anything different how was I to know what was right and what was wrong? But I did not like what was happening to me and I had no one to tell. My mother always told me that kids should be seen and not heard and if you were heard you were told to shut up.

Sometimes I just want to scream out so loud but will people even hear me or understand me? The shit I've been through I really want to explain and talk about, it haunts me each and every day. It has angered me and it was not okay what I had to face and keep my mouth shut thinking that it was normal.

I lost my virginity at the tender age of twelve. I remember it like yesterday. Wham bam thank you mam, no longer than a second. I call it the two-second stroke because it wasn't intercourse but in two strokes he had taken my virginity.

As kids you fondle around trying out things and that's what I tried. I didn't know what the hell I was doing but I did it anyway, my legs shaking, blood flowing down my legs. I never knew I had lost my virginity until a few years later when it was time for our sex education class and the conversation was about how you lose your virginity and that was when I knew, oh my god I had lost mine, nothing romantic about it. Nothing was taught to me so I didn't know any different. I wish I'd waited for that special person, that special moment. You know, a girl's dream: rose petals on the bed, soft mellow music, making love, good and happy times with good memories. I did it all wrong and rushed the one thing I should have cherished.

I became more intrigued about sex and was fondling around with boys, but no sexual penetration until I was seventeen years of age.

That was Sunni's special moment. I met Sunni at the YMCA in Watford on a youth program. He liked me as soon as he saw me and we hit it off straight away. He asked me out and I was kind of shy but I said yes a few months later. We dated for around two years on and off until we departed and called an end to our relationship. Well, I kind of messed up our relationship. Not being honest and genuine and loving cost me the love of a good person. But I will never forget that day. I class that day as the first time I had intercourse and it was amazing.

One day after school when I was about thirteen I went to the local off-licence and bought the biggest cider bottle. I drank the whole thing before I got to the funfair. By the time I got into the funfair I was paralytic drunk from drinking old English cider, passing out in Burnt Oak park while the funfair continued and the locals kids screamed on the rides enjoying their fun day out with their families. The colourful lights were a blur as I lay on the grass, head spinning, wishing I had stayed at home.

The shit I got up to was utter madness, an experience I never want my daughter to have. It wasn't nice being a young girl, vulnerable on the streets of London. Most of the time I was with my older brother Leonardo. He gave me weed and alcohol by the time I was fourteen. I was more enthusiastic about smoking and drinking but my brain was not able to hack the strong chemicals. What a caring brother I had.

He finds those things amusing which I find strange. He enjoys seeing others drunk or high. I can't explain why he's this way. He didn't do me justice growing up, he should have protected me not lure me into devastation. Sometimes I think to myself, is there a ulterior motive behind my brother luring me into drink and drugs?

I rebelled so much in my school that I ended up in a school centre for troubled kids, the Pavilion Centre in Whetstone. This is where I blossomed immensely. I actually loved the school; they listened and taught you instead of telling you what to do. I wasn't a person who liked to be told what to do and if you tried to control me I would rebel. I'm still this way, I can't stand controlling people it irritates me beyond belief. I did drama at the Pavilion and yet again I was outstanding. Alistair was my drama teacher. He was of slim build with ginger hair, a tiny man but lovely. He knew his shit when it came to drama. He'd also taught me drama at Edgware School so we hit it off as soon as he saw me. He always wanted me to become an actress and pursue my dream. He would tell me, "Katrina," in his Scottish voice, "you are so lovely please stay focused. You are exceptional and articulate. As an actress you will go far." Alistair saw potential in me but when you're lost, you're lost. In my own little world I could hear him but I was not able to listen. I was too far gone by then and there was no turning back. Alistair begged me to stay off the streets, begged me to keep focused but he didn't know what I was facing at home. I passed my GCSEs and of course I came out with an A for Drama and Art. Creativity is in my soul, it's natural. I was gifted with this and with an easy charm and a down-to-earth, easy-going personality. People just can't resist me and now I know why. I'm loyal, honest and good to be around; the life of the party.

What I have come to understand is that people will see your shine, beauty and blessings and will want to take your shine, beauty and blessings without realising your blessings are for you. People are so lost within themselves that they look for an escape and you might be that for them. Be mindful, people can dampen your shine and block your blessings. Never lose focus on where you're going and what you're doing. Strive through and through. Let nobody distract you from your journey. High school was a challenging time I didn't know where I was heading but I went along with whatever crossed my path.

Me at Hendon High School, my first school photo

CHAPTER 5
MY LIFE WAS IN DANGER

Imagine someone trying to kill you, and the reason is because you were born and breathing.

I used the analogy of kill because if you like or love something you should not want to destroy it, and if you try to destroy something eventually it dies.

Imagine they want to see you in the gutter, not wanting to see you prosper, not wanting to see you progress because of their own demons. People are so damaged that they want to damage other people and they get satisfaction from watching people's lives self-destruct, or they find ways to block your blessings. All I can say to the people who have tried to kill me is I really feel so sorry for you, it must feel so painful to see me live and there's nothing you can do about it.

I walk with God and he always walks with me.

I don't really want to talk about this, I've wasted enough of my life on people that are irrelevant to me and to put them in my book is not something I really wanted to do but it's a part of my life so I must talk of my experiences in order for you to understand what my life is and was about.

Me and Leonardo found out we were brother and sister at his birthday party, he would have been about fourteen at the time. I had called Leonardo my cousin for years until that fateful day. It all came out that I was Ronald's daughter. I was none the wiser as to who my dad was. Growing up I was a part of both families. I had been going to Leonardo's house from the time I was a baby and was welcomed in the family home. My family knew his family and it ran deep; my mum, uncles and aunties all went to school with Leonardo's family and this is why we called one another cousins. They were all friends.

THE LOVE OF A MOTHER

My mum told me Ronald came to her house on her sixteenth birthday with a couple of friends and gave her drink and drugs and had his wicked way with her. Being young and coming from a home that was always in turmoil and being unprotected and rebellious, Ronald wormed his way in with my mum and told her that he and his girlfriend were no longer together. This was untrue, but no matter what was said I'm here to tell the story.

Once it was established I was Ronald's daughter, Leonardo and me were told and that was it, we were told to get on with it. No one explained anything to me and Leonardo and this is where all the problems began. My brother's mum switched on me like I fucked her man. I found it very confusing. I was at my brother's house every day from the time I had been born then all of a sudden she would give me evil looks and would tell Leonardo, "Don't bring that bitch back in my house." Why? I thought. What have I done wrong? I was only ten, what had I done to deserve this?

I'm going to tell you a story and believe me you're going to be shocked but it's a true story and I went through it, still living to tell the tale. I was still going to my brother's house after all the commotion about me but I didn't know his mum was bitter and twisted. She couldn't stand the fact that I was born. My mother forced me to communicate with Ronald and I told her aged ten I wasn't interested, in fact I told her I never wanted him in my life, but she continued to push it.

One day my mum told me it was father's day. I couldn't care less, I had never in my life bought a father's day card and I just wanted to play out with my friends like every other day. She was going on and on, "Buy him a card and post it to his house." Why she would want me to do that I don't know but I thought that was nuts. Maybe she wanted to start some trouble, who knows. She made me buy a card from our local corner shop and go up to his home and post it. What a wrong move that was. Leonardo's mum went crazy and who got the blame? Yes me, the young innocent girl who didn't give two shits about her so-called father. Ronald came down to my house, not to see me or bring me food or to see if I was okay, he came down to tell me to never do that again. I said,

"Okay." I wasn't fussed. I didn't want him in my life anyway. He was doing me a favour to be honest. The only people I cared about were my uncles, aunts and cousins on my mother's side; they were important to me, I spent most of my time with them.

Ronald continued to take the piss not being there for me but being there for Leonardo and other people's children. It never affected me, what you can't see won't hurt you, but I would hear of what he was doing for others. What was pissing me off was the puppy show he would do to make out to other people he was looking after me. I blame my mum for that, she should have told him to fuck off and leave me alone but she was weak and it showed.

There were many days my brother would pick me up from my home and we would spend the day and time together but on this day he picked me up and needed to pass his home to collect something. He went into his bedroom and I went into the living room. I went and sat on the sofa putting the television on. From the corner of my eye in the middle of the fireplace I saw a picture of me with Voodoo beads around it. I didn't know at the time what they were but now I know and if I'd known at the time I would have taken my picture and thrown the beads away in Burnt Oak Silkstream River with no return. How did she get my picture? I wondered. Some scary shit thinking about it now, but my mum told me that she dabbles in witchcraft and they had done it when they were kids before all the madness happened.

Soon after I saw the beads around my picture my brother asked for me and our cousin Jevene to stay over at his house. For some strange reason Leonardo's mum agreed. She ignored me the whole time I was there. It felt so funny, one of the most horrible experiences as a child I have ever felt, staying somewhere you're not welcome. Anyway I stayed and went home the next day in one piece. Well, just about. As soon as I got home I was so sick I nearly died, she had given me some kind of food that was not good. I don't know if it was poison or food poisoning but let me tell you I was projectile vomiting, running to the toilet weak as hell not making it because I was so weak, my mum wiping my ass because I was so weak, carrying me onto the chair. I was uncontrollably shaking with hot and cold sweats. It was terrible. I was the only one sick. How did that happen? I swear we ate the same food and Jevene was fine and Leonardo was fine. And that's when I knew this mad woman wanted to kill me.

Once I recovered I refused to go to her house, she was a fruit loop. Only a sick individual could do such a terrible thing. I felt let down by my mother for putting me in danger knowing full well what that woman was capable of doing. I was vexed.

It doesn't stop there. I was coming home from Hendon School on December 6th 1997 with my friend Pretty. It was a cold winter's night and it was our friend Carla Smith's birthday. She'd turned fourteen and we were so excited to see her. Carla went to Edgware School which I ended up attending a year later. Rushing to Carla's house we knocked on the door. Her mum answered, "Carla's not back from school yet," so we decided to go to Pretty's house so she could tell her parents where we were going and change our school clothes. Crossing the Edgware Road, West Hendon Broadway, I bumped into Leonardo's auntie, Sharon. She was happy to see me. We spoke and she told me to take care and walked into the pound shop. As I turned to my left in the car was Leonardo's mum staring at me with the deepest stare. Thinking of it now brings shivers down my spine; you could see the evil in her eyes. From the look on her face alone I knew there were no good intentions, she was thinking pure evil. But it didn't faze me. I didn't care about her; I was a young girl living my life. I don't even know why she was so pissed, it's not as if Ronald was looking after me.

Me and Pretty crossed the road and walked down towards my home to tell my mum where we were going. My mum was okay, she liked Pretty and Carla and she could see how excited we were. She told me not to be too late home. Happy we got the OK we walked towards Pretty's home, a couple of seconds walk away from my home.

We got to the road waiting to cross. We saw the traffic slowing down so we walked out looking both ways. There was a single lane to the left, it looked clear. We quickly ran out and then BANG! In almost a split second we were hit by a speeding car. The bang was so loud you could hear the echo all over the west Hendon estate. I flew into the air landing on my back; Pretty hit the bonnet of the car and landed a couple of metres from me. Was I still alive I thought feeling very serial & not understand what had just happened? Blurry lights ahead started to fade. I could see Pretty trying to stand up holding her back as I lay on the cold floor. "Is she okay?" I thought I heard the screams of a woman over me. "Oh my god I didn't see them! Oh my god are they okay?" Hand over her mouth, tears streaming down her face. I think she was in more shock than me.

My mother's friend Jackie rushed over to me as she returned home from work in disbelief at what she was seeing. Jackie ran to get my mum. I remember my mum screaming, bolting across the road. It was the first time I had ever seen my mother fight for me. I actually thought wow, she cares. She really wanted to kill the driver of the car, calling her all sorts of names. "Stupid bitch can't you see?"

The poor woman's response was so shakey as she spoke tears streaming down her face as she was so apologetic, "I'm sorry they just ran out in the road."

While I lay on the road only one thought came to mind: prior to the accident I had just seen that wicked witch. Did she actually cause this accident? In my heart of hearts I believe she put wickedness on me and it's a shame Pretty got into the mix.

That was it for me, I told my mum, "I never want to be around that woman, she's a vile and cruel woman who has wicked intentions."

To this day when I see her I'm fuming. I never asked to be born. She couldn't challenge my mother or Ronald but tackled an innocent child. This is how I know she's weak. There's so much more to tell but I don't want to spend my time talking about horrible things, it has no value but I will not hide wicked people.

This is why I think my brother has or had a ulterior motive towards our relationship. You have to remember she is still his mother. How else could she get to me? The easiest way was through my brother. Maybe I'm paranoid but who knows. You cannot blame me. If someone tried to kill you how would you feel?

After the accident Pretty and I came out with not a scratch on our heads. By the grace of God he had protected us from evil.

We had two weeks off school with ice cream, magazines and pampering from my over-caring mum, uncles and aunts. I missed school but they wouldn't allow us to go in after a traumatic incident. We had to rest up.

I believe things happen in life for a reason. I don't care how she feels about me, I don't care what she says about me but I do care if she tries to harm me and my family. I do not trust her and I will never trust her. If she can do that to an innocent child, who knows who else she can cause harm to.

I do believe there are wicked people in this world. I do not associate myself with those kinds of people, my heart is pure and I fear nothing.

CHAPTER 6
FIGHT LIKE A MAN

At about the age of fourteen I started fighting, getting in trouble. I became notorious for fighting in school, fighting out of school; I was just an angry child.

I got into a few fights and made a name for myself. "Oh, Katrina. Don't mess with her she'll beat you up, she's hard. You don't want to have it with her." What's crazy is I was soft as a marshmallow but this was how I was raised: don't let no one trouble you and if they did smack 'em up. If I didn't I would get smacked up by my brother so I had no choice but to fight and I started to like it. The anger gives you some kind of power or a rush that people fear you, but it can also get you used and into a lot of trouble.

I was also fed up of the abuse I was facing at home, so if someone was rude to me or even looked at me in the wrong way they were going to get it and I wasn't fucking about. I would give them what they deserved, well, what I thought they deserved and that was it. But it was wrong, completely wrong.

I was expelled from Edgware School for knocking a girl out and breaking her nose. Yet again it was no fault of mine, listening to these people who knew my triggers. You look at me I will switch up on you; you dare confront me I'm beating you down. I was savage. No talking just POW and you're knocked out.

I'm not proud of fighting but that was all I knew and was taught to do: don't take any shit. But taking no shit sometimes comes with shit. My friend Lisa had a friend called Hayley, she became friends with her when she moved back to Hendon, but Hayley would always get herself into a problem and she would call Lisa; not me because we weren't friends. Every time Lisa and me were chilling Hayley would call with some sort of problem and we'd go fight for her. I, like a damn fool, I would go thinking I was being a friend for Lisa and who would end up fighting? Me. I didn't clock at first what was happening until Hayley was going out partying with her white friends but leaving me and Lisa behind, then Lisa would get a call and boom, we were off beating up and rushing girls. A few times we beat up some girls and it all started with Hayley, Lisa following and me the ass following suit.

It didn't click until one day when we were roaming the streets as we usually did. I didn't really hang with Lisa much but I would spend time with Lisa, Hayley and the rest of the Sims. We did have fun times when Hayley had birthday parties at her home but that's all we were allowed to no other event; keep the blacks quiet and behind closed doors. Standing by Colindale Station a group of us were chilling out. Hayley whispered something to Lisa and the next thing I knew Lisa ran off after a girl who had just walked past us. I didn't even see the girl I was so in my own little bubble. The next thing I see, POW! Lisa hit the girl and they began to fight. I went running over no questions asked. POW! I hit the girl I could have killed her. She hit the floor and we started to rush the poor girl. I saw a brick and picked it up and was just about to hit the girl with the brick when it was pulled from my hand. "Don't do it." Coming back to my senses in the midst of the commotion I stopped and thought what am I doing? I took a step back and looked at Hayley laughing at the girl, not even laying a finger on the girl who apparently attacked her.

That was it for me. After that night I pulled myself away from them. I felt like I was being used and they genuinely weren't my friends, but only wanted me around for fighting and stupidity.

Lisa still hung around with Hayley and the girls but I started moving further and further away but not into anything better, just smoking, drinking and chilling more with my boy Stewart Sheridan. Even though Stewart and me got into mischief it wasn't bad stuff we were doing. I liked Stewart's company; he is loyal, funny and very loving. They always say when you bring other friends into the mix it can cause jealously and I definitely know this.

I started moving back with Stewart. I won't disclose what we got up to because it's Stewart's business. If he wants to express his story that's up to him but what I will say is we went on tour around London city and on our journey laughed, joked and enjoyed life. Some of my best moments were with Stewart, he will always remain my good friend. I will always be there for him no matter what. That's a friendship that is genuine; he doesn't have a bad bone in his body. I value his friendship very much.

Stewy and me grew up together from a young age on the West Hendon estate. My mother and Stew's mum became good friends when they were growing up on the estate and history just repeated itself with me and Stewart, but the cycle has ended with my generation. My daughter will not feel that same freedom I did, the community love and togetherness. Blacks, English, Irish and Asians were united and we somehow got along and respected each other. With all the racism in the world we made a community from love and we grew with this. I will keep those memories close to my heart. I do miss the good times we used to have. Life was so different and happy but I will not take the memories of fighting and conflict I got myself into, that is a past memory that I want to move on from and start with a fresh mind of love and peace.

CHAPTER 7
MOTHER WHY CAN'T YOU HEAR ME?

The first time my mother threw me out onto the streets I was fourteen years of age. Anything I did: "Get out of my house!" Sometimes I didn't even do anything, but when she met my brother's dad I was constantly thrown out on the street so she could spend her nights with a man I knew nothing about. He was some Ghanaian man called Peter who was married and had his family living a few miles away. "Go get out my house, go to Lisa's," was a regular record I used to hear. I was very surprised my mother dated a black man, she can't stand black people or black men and is very offensive towards them. Me and my family often make jokes towards the comments my mother makes, we will frequently say I should have been born mixed race with lovely curly hair and jet blue eyes.

My mother has a special saying; she wished she were a white woman. Believe me she definitely does wish she were a white woman, her way of talking alone and her mannerisms and how she talks about her black race. I bet when she looks in the mirror she sees a white lady with blonde hair and blue eyes. My mother is a top Gary like them black boys dissing black girls for the white race. Me, I'm very proud to be black; the blacker the better. I respect everybody but I will never disrespect my race for another, that's just insane.

My mother was drinking and smoking, going out partying all night, having all kinds of people in the house. The house stank of weed and alcohol was spread all over the table. I felt neglected but the one thing my mother would make sure of was that I would eat and I had clothes on my back. My mother was just a faint memory. She was there but not mentally. The feeling that I had no mother was the norm. I had to grow up very fast. I was way out of control, a lost soul lost in the system. Now

I know my behaviour was not bad, it was a cry for help, a cry no one was hearing. You see if my mother had opened her mind instead of dwelling on past events that were out of her control, she could have listened to my cries from within.

It's a painful thought when you crave a mother's enduring love and don't receive a smidge of it in return. It can make you bitter.

I have a vague vision of that decade in my life, and I can only remember certain events. I have tried my best to remember why my mother was not listening to me. Why was she ignoring me? My mind goes blank and straight back to happier thoughts. They say painful memories are usually pushed so far to the back of your mind that you forget them completely. I have asked my cousin on many occasions about events that have occurred and I would struggle to remember the incidents that happened, I guess that's a good thing, troubled memories can hold you down mentally.

I know my mother would have liked to be heard when she was young, and needed assistance. She constantly reminds each and every single family member. I will never get to grips why she treated me the way her father treated her.

The circle of life continues because we never allow ourselves freedom. Freedom from ourselves, freedom from our minds, freedom from the past, freedom from life.

It is important to set yourself free.

Me as an individual, the person you shall seek is the person you shall find, within spirituality and within soul. Its crazy how life experiences can change you forever, knocking you back to size, questioning all the things you have done in your life.

I'm such an easy going person I love me. I do question why has my life been so tough

Throughout my life I had nothing but heartbreak; the worst part is the love of a mother. If I had the love of my mother nothing in life could faze me. I would feel safe, protected and loved but I felt alone and unwanted. Why didn't my mother love me?

THE LOVE OF A MOTHER

Why is it so difficult for parents to understand their children? To communicate with my mother I find it very hard and tiring. If I need to express myself, my emotions, my concerns, the things I'm going through, the last person I would ask for assistance would be my mother. I would not be able to console with my mother for emotional support as she is very cold and does not know how to comfort me, love me, or nurture me. My mother will never understand how I feel mentally and physically. Instead of her dictating rules and regulations on how she feels I should live my life she should see the positive in me and encourage me to have an outstanding future. My mother has a negative outlook on where I'm heading with my future accomplishments and she is unwilling to understand me or engage with me. My voice is unheard. When I was crying out for help my cries were ignored and my mother believed I would be a child forever in mind and body, but the circle of life makes our minds and bodies grow into mature adults, who then have children of our own and the circle of life continues. She has tried her best to suppress my way of thinking as I'm a very rebellious person and if I show you respect I would definitely want respect in return. I wish my mother knew who her daughter was and maybe she would have respect for me, being a mother with a young daughter myself. My mother is not someone I need in my life but I give my mother that respect as she's my mother. A mother is very important in a child's existence because she is the life line, a parent and a child's relationship should be very special, it is of truth and honour.

I'm regularly analyzing and thinking why does my mother have so much hatred in her heart towards me?

CHAPTER 8
THE PARTY LIFE

The first time I had a drink in a pub I was fifteen. Lisa and I were introduced to the Hendon Pub by Mick, Hayley's father. Mick recently passed away from prostate cancer in November 2017. Hayley and her family were kind enough to let me see Mick for one last time before he passed away. He was such a lovely man, God rest his soul. When Mick invited Lisa and me to the Hendon pub it was for some lunch, which was very nice of him, but from that day Lisa and me would make that our regular party spot. We started raving from a young age but most people did. My mother definitely did and I just followed suit. Being in a pub became something normal for me. Whenever our parents would ask where we were going we would say we were staying at each other's houses. Our parents would not even check in with each other to see if we were lying, and we definitely were lying; we were out raving. Often we had school in the morning and somehow we made it in the next day all raved out, stinking like a brewery.

The 90s were a peak time and my emotions got the better of me: a young teenager drinking, smoking and roaming the streets. I didn't touch cocaine until I was seventeen and only took ecstasy twice, but it was a small phase I went through. Cocaine is not a drug for me to be honest, weed yes, but not cocaine; I call it the devil man drug and weed the black man herb. Not skunk, that Arab chemical nonsense, the plant weed, a natural herb with natural healing which is good for the mind, body and soul if you boil it and drink it.

So our parents thought we were safely sleeping at one of our houses. Personally I don't think my mother really gave two shits where we were as long as we were out of the house. Lisa's mum was a bit different, her mother would want her home and she wasn't allowed out often, but as she got older her mother trusted her more. Lisa was a quiet girl at home and a wild girl on the streets. That's what made her mother trust her, she thought Lisa was a quiet little girl not knowing she was notorious out there, fighting, drinking and… well, you can figure out the rest.

I raved from the age of fifteen till the age of twenty-three and when I tell you we raved, we raved. We started pub crawling. The Welsh Harp pub had some good garage nights and everyone from West Hendon would be there. We would rave in the Hendon pub, from there to Pochines, from Pochines to Courts Wine Bar and raving all over London. Temple was one of our regular party spots. Garage raves were in at that time and we were young and free to do what we wanted and we did just that.

There were a few times we got into a bit of trouble but nothing we couldn't handle, a few sticky situations and trusting people too much. God definitely had his hands covered over me in certain situations. After some incidents I'm surprised I'm still living. I really loved growing up in the 90s, there was so much freedom, less crime and fewer people in the country. I just wish I'd had the mentality that I have now; I would have handled situations much better.

Even though I lied to my mother about where I was staying she was fully aware I was out raving and she didn't care whether I returned home or not. I remember a time, it was a very hot summer's day and I was walking home. I bumped into Lisa's mum. "Hi Katcheen," as she called me.

"Hi."

"Where you off to?"

"Home."

"I have to meet my friend later, would you like to come?"

"Nah not really."

"It's only for a few hours then we'll be back. You might as well, you're not doing anything are you?"

I eventually gave in and went. This is where I learned a lot about going with your feelings; if you don't want to do something don't do it.

Anyway, we ended up travelling and meeting some random guy. I said to myself what the hell have I done? My uncle is going to kill me. We ended up down a pub and then going back to the man's home. I slept on the sofa and Helen was upstairs with the man.

The next morning I woke up and I was ready to go. I headed up the stairs and I knocked on the bedroom door. "Come in."

"Helen I've got to go home."

"Okay let me see the times for the trains." They had been cancelled. Not only did she take me on a dangerous trip to meet men off the internet, she'd left her two young boys at home alone and told them to not answer the door or the phone. Helen had planned to stay there for two days and didn't let me know. What madness. This is why it is very important for mothers and fathers to be active in their children's lives, or they will end up feeling worthless and vulnerable and people will take advantage of their vulnerability.

My mother was ringing and ringing but Helen was lying and making her way out of the situation. She'd wanted to satisfy her own needs but she needed company. I don't know why she didn't take her own daughter with her, but she kept her daughter out of danger and put me in it.

After spending the night there I was adamant I needed to get home but we had to wait for our train. In the meantime the hospitality was nice. We were treated nicely and with respect but he was a racist and boy did I know it; he had Helen in his phone as 'darkie'. He wanted to sleep with a black woman just to see what it was like. A fantasy he maybe thought about.

Eventually after a few hours it was time for our train and I couldn't wait to get home. That's when I knew this was crazy and I needed to give Lisa and Helen a break. When I returned home I started rolling with other people and my brother more. That was a wake-up call for me and I never put myself in a situation like that again, that was a big lesson for me to learn and I really learned my lesson.

As the raving started to die down I started finding myself a bit and knew what I kind of wanted. Raving was getting boring for me and I wanted to see the world. Things had started to get out of control: Lisa and me ended up getting into a car crash that nearly killed us, we were meeting all kinds of men, our drinks being spiked. That was it for me. I knew then I wanted something different and I wanted out of this mess. It started to become messy when Lisa was speaking of my personal affairs to any and everybody about my abortions and me taking cocaine, I feel that is very disrespectful. Luckily I have a few people that have my back and Lisa was unaware who these people were but they were keeping me updated as to who Lisa really was and she was not a true friend to me. Everyone kept telling me to keep away from her, but my loyalty still remained and we had known each other for a long time. I guess who can't hear must feel and boy did I feel it. You see people talk about other people so they can distract themselves from their true character so people will focus on you. When you're a vibrant, confident character people will feel intimidated by your presence, so if people speak bad of you it makes them feel good. But with me what you see is what you get and that makes me true. I have nothing to hide, never will and never have.

I think what topped it for me is when they accused me of stealing and that was it for me. I used to class Lisa and her mother as family but nah, that's not even a true friend let alone family. That was very hurtful and for someone like me when I take you as a friend I take all of you, loyal to the end. I would never take something without asking and that's what hurts the most, they never really knew me. Thirty years of friendship just thrown away. And if they felt I did do it just ask me and I will tell you, but don't go bashing my name and still looking in my face like we're cool. I don't play those games and I never will.

I respect her and her family. I have never stolen and would never steal from them. Our friendship will never be the same again, I see things differently now.

I am friends with a few old school friends and we keep in contact. I don't call people my friends unless I believe you're truly a friend. I do have a few people that I know I can trust and are 100% loyal. They passed the loyalty test. It's very sad that you have to check who is who because people can't be trusted.

We had some outstanding moments that do make me feel sad. We grew up happy and having fun but our journeys are going in different directions and I wish her all the best for the future. I had great times with Lisa and her family from the 80s to the 2000s and I will hold those memories tight in my heart, memories you cannot get again. That chapter is over and now it's time for a new chapter with a new beginning.

CHAPTER 9
SWEET SIXTEEN

Turning sixteen was an eventful time for me. I was going through puberty, growing up fast, finding my way in life. By this time I had a different mindset. I was completely confused about life and was trying to find my way to get through.

Lying in my bed, I would stare into the sky at night, smile and think about how my life was going to be when I grew up, and I would move far away from all the pain and suffering, move away from all the wicked people around me. I would have my own family and I would love and cherish them forever. But that didn't go to plan.

I struggled in life and when I would look in the mirror all I would see was my mother. I would wish my face would open up like a flower and blossom. Am I like my mum? The same smile, the same laugh, do we walk the same? And when people say "Ooh Katrina you look like your mum," I get my back up in an instant. But I do look like my mum, I know I do. I see it and I have some of her characteristics and traits.

I look at other mothers and I think do they treat their children the same? Then I wonder how the hell did this woman get away with treating me in such a way and no one even blinked an eyelid.

My mother was mentally abusing me. I never knew what mental abuse was, but I knew something was wrong; what I was facing could never be normal behaviour. And now she tells me years later, "You know when you have a child for a guy and he disses you, well yeah, you can look at your child and take out all your anger on your child. Your child is a constant reminder of that pain and hurtful feelings." Okay so it's bad enough being hated by the world, now even your own mother dislikes you, how great is that?

I was so confused by my mother's behaviour that it made me sick and

I would constantly think that I was the problem. I guess I was to a degree but I really thought I had done things wrong. She would burst into my room while I was sleeping at 3am, drunk and screaming, swaying from side to side. I'd see a blur in front of me. Half asleep I'd see someone in my face. Trying to compose myself, rubbing my eyes to see clearly I'd see my drunken mother standing in my face. "You slut, you whore, why haven't you washed the dishes?" Jumping up, scaring me to the point I stopped sleeping and would stay up until she drank herself to sleep after blasting her music throughout the night.

The looks my mother would give me could scare anyone around her. She was so violent, so strange, so angry. Her mood was unpredictable and when she wasn't drinking, or certain people were around, I got the best sleep. It was crazy. The only time I felt I could sleep was if someone was in the house. It used to fucking vex me because all I wanted was a normal life. Why was it so hard to be happy? I promised myself once I was older I would never speak to my mother again.

So much abuse, so much hate, frustrating beyond belief. With all the madness going on I got my first job at Premier House in Edgware as a telesales consultant. I was so excited. Lisa got the job at the same time as me and we worked together. We would catch so many jokes, the fun we had, and the laughter was constant in the office. Most of the people who worked there all went to school together and I never wanted to go home.

Now I was working I had to start paying my way, my mother wanted twenty pounds a week for gas and electric, my job never lasted long. I was tired and ratty from the abuse I was receiving at home so I said fuck it what's the point of working when I can't get no sleep, no peace, no love. I should have used my head and saved up my money to get myself a secure home and start a fresh life, a new beginning, a new journey where no one knew me. I could live happily ever after in peace.

All I wanted was one day for someone to just come and take me away, and to live in a lovely house with lovely parents and get a good night's sleep. That would never happen for me, I would cry on my knees and ask God, "Can you hear me? Why can't my mother hear me? Why is she doing this to me? What have I done?" But no one heard my cries.

CHAPTER 10
WATFORD: THE YMCA

I ended up on the social but not for long; I loved working and making my own money. Partying and roaming the streets drinking, smoking, doing things a sixteen year-old young girl should not be doing. I should have been at home in bed. Suddenly an opportunity arose for me to go to college in Watford at the YMCA. I jumped at the chance; maybe this was my break, my way out, a fresh start in life. I applied and got accepted into the college. I was overwhelmed. Surely there was no way I could fuck this up?

Our mentor was called Harry Charles. If you Google Harry you will see his information, he has done many good things for children who are and were vulnerable, helping and guiding them on their journey to a better future, Anthony Joshua being one of them.

That cold winter Friday morning I walked up the stairs, I felt like I was walking forever. The room where we had to meet was right at the top. When I reached the top all eyes were on me, I was the last to arrive. "Hello," I said quickly like I was shy but they didn't know this girl was one fucking rebel with a no caring attitude. Most of the kids on there were going through some sort of shit and I had met my match on this course. Most kids were trouble and came from a troubled past. We introduced ourselves; everyone was on his or her best behaviour, everyone being nice. We were told there and then we were going away, I can't remember where we went but it was somewhere on the coast, a beautiful place. We hadn't known each other for five minutes and now we were going to be spending the week living together. All kinds of emotions ran through my mind: excitement, nerves, happiness, but all I could think about was that I wanted to get a good night's sleep. I hadn't had a good night's sleep since my grandmother was alive. I was always on edge when I was left with my mother alone.

There would be no one bursting into my room at 3am frightening me out of my sleep, shouting and screaming at me. I might get a little lie-in, which would feel amazing. Maybe I could lie there forever and dream the pain away.

This was where I met Sunni Hoodli, the nice guy. This is one of the memories I will never forget; it sticks in my mind. Someone who actually liked me for me, something I never understood.

There was a group of us on this trip including our mentor Harry Charles. I don't remember all the names of the people on the trip, but I bonded with Sunni, Ryan, Billy and a few girls. The day before I got my hair done at the salon to make myself look pretty, not knowing we were going on an adventure trip with activities like mud climbing, canoeing, swimming in the sea, jumping off cliffs; you name it we did it, and living on a farm. But I guess my hair caught the eye of the blued-eyed, blond, shaved hair young man Sunni Hoodli. He was so nice to me and liked me for me. We got along straight away. The drive up to the farm was really nice. I wanted to sit with Harry but I wasn't allowed for health and safety reasons so I sat with Sunni. We spoke there and he said my hair was nice, smiling, looking directly into my eyes. I was shocked. How could he actually like me? I wondered what he saw when he looked at me.

After a six hour drive, tired and exhausted, we finally got to the farm. Throwing our bags down on the front porch there was no one to be seen. Harry walked around looking for the farm owners so they could let us in. "Hi!" we heard from a distance. Everyone turned to look in the dark. Coming towards us was an old man and his wife. "We thought you got lost." We reassured them no, it was just a long drive. I picked up my bag with low energy from tiredness and we made our way into the farm. I placed myself at the table where everyone was told to sit. Putting my bag down I rubbed my face and spread my arms out over the table, head faced down. I wanted to sleep; all I wanted to do was sleep. We had a long day ahead the next day. Harry shouted as I lifted up my head,

"Everyone pick your rooms." I wanted to sleep alone in a room that was so tiny. There was a small bed but that was it, nothing could get in there. I didn't know how to socialise and how to behave around other people let alone sleep in the same room for a week. My mind was fucked, I would shun people, I just wanted to be alone, sleep alone, be all by myself and get a good night's sleep. "Sleep with the girls Katrina," Harry whispered to me. "What's wrong? Why do you want to sleep alone in the little room full of cobwebs, spiders and dust?" I started to see Harry could pick up on my insecurities.

"No reason, I've just never shared a room before," I said, smiling to take the nerves away. "Aaaarrrggh okay then," I muttered. I had no choice, I was thrown in the deep end, something I could not control. How was I going to cope? Typical. Someone was being nice to me and I clammed up, not knowing how to act. For fuck's sake Katrina get a grip, but I just couldn't do it, the mental scars stayed in my head. What if they don't like me, what if I'm too much, what if I make a fool of myself then everyone's going to laugh at me. To make it easy I will be the clown, I will make a joke out of myself then it's okay, we can all laugh at me together.

I could hear the strange sounds of the cows mooing in the early morning with the fresh air and green grass; I could live there no problem. From the distance I could see as I blinked my eyes the beautiful sunbeams shining through the window. I could not believe it, I'd slept through the night so peacefully, one of the best sleeps I'd had in a long time. Looking over at the other beds the rest of them were still asleep. Going downstairs to the toilet I bumped into Sunni. "Good morning."

"Morning," I replied, "how come you're up so early?"

"I can ask the same question." Sunni was always talking to me and on my case, me not knowing he liked me. I just thought oh shut up will ya.

"What's for breakfast?" he said. I looked at him not saying a word but in my head thinking it's too early for this it's 6am for goodness' sake.

We sat at the table talking. Sunni made us both a cup of tea and we chilled out. Then other faces appeared. By 7:30am everyone was up, breakfast being made, people in the shower getting ready for the day ahead. "Is everyone ready?" Harry shouted out. "Come on let's get going we have a busy schedule ahead."

Making our way to the minibus Sunni escorted me on and sat next to me. We laughed and joked, taking in the country air and scenery. I class our trip as our first holiday. He would laugh if I said this but this was where we were so happy and he made me happy, we got on so well. I liked jungle music and listened to this a lot growing up and so did he. He brought his Walkman on the trip and we would listen to it together, laughing and rocking our heads back and forth. I think he was shocked when I told him I listened to jungle. I bet he was thinking I listened to Bob Marley because I'm black. Well I do but that's not all I listen to.

I sit here now as I'm writing this and I reminisce the way he would look at me, the way he was with me. If only I humbled myself and took my time to love him. The way he looked and was so loving towards me… I wonder what would have been?

Sunni was so gentle and so nice to me, only God knows how I could fuck up something so good.

We reached our destination all excited and ready to go, we were canoeing in the river. I think Harry was more scared than we were; one man on a trip with twenty rebellious kids in the river, how the hell was he going to do this? But he did and we all respected and listened to him, he spoke to us in a way that we liked. He made us understand life.

I was still a bit shy and never showed my full potential but everyone was nice and we all got on. If someone was struggling we would help one another, which was nice. We were learning life skills. The day was long, wet and eventful. We managed to canoe around the river, no one fell in, no one was harmed and we had the best fun. We got back to shore and darkness was setting in, it was time to head back. Harry said, "Get all your stuff, pack it away and place it back in the cloakroom." By now we were all hungry, tired and wanted to get back. It was another long drive. When we arrived back it was pitch black, and we were self catering so there was no dinner prepared. No one thought to go shopping and buy food; I blame Harry for this, he should have just brought something that we could make for the week. I didn't know how to shop, I didn't even know how to cook. Yes a seventeen year-old girl did not know how to cook. Well if it's never taught to you how are you supposed to know? Somehow food was rustled up; one of the girls found tuna and peppers and other stuff, I think they asked our neighbours for some ingredients as well. Whatever it was we had food for the night, but our night was not over. I brought weed on the trip and by now we had all bonded and we were all getting along. Another girl also brought weed so we were in happy times. We went out to the fields and smoked our night away. As the night continued we wanted to explore the area, it was me, Sunni, Ryan and Tolla. As high as we were we wanted to get higher and find a pub. To our amazement walking down the road we found a mini pub. We all had money on us and we all went to get a drink, but Sunni was rejected. "Why?" he said. "I'm eighteen."

"No you're not," the barman replied, "you look fifteen. Do you have ID?" I didn't know Sunni was actually sixteen, one year younger than me. All of us were baffled and shocked. We left the pub and went back to the farm, laughing and joking outside. I sat on Sunni's lap and he placed his arms around me and we kissed, not shy anyone. After a few hours of chatting and being noisy Harry came downstairs. "Come on guys you have to be up early. Bed." Sunni and me had other plans. Ryan and Tolla went up to bed while Sunni and me stayed downstairs. It was 1am.

"You know I like you." Sunni stared into my eyes. Feeling shy and out of place I looked away. Lifting my head back up he looked into my eyes deeply and drew in for a kiss. It was like the big bang, that's all I felt inside, a big bang. Locking our lips together we engaged in a passionate kiss. The way he touched me made me feel a whole gamut of emotions but I felt really nice. "Will you be my girlfriend?" he said as he slowly kissed my lips. Frozen from fear of saying the wrong thing, I started to kiss him back to distract him from asking me to be his girlfriend again. Tongues a-flow he started to rub his hands down the side of my thighs, around and in-between my legs. He gently laid me down on the sofa and we lay there enjoying one another, pleasuring while he took my clothes off, gradually taking off his clothes. What was I doing? Katrina, I said to myself, you hardly know him think about what you're about to do. You know when your conscience is troubling you, you know it's so wrong but yet feels so right.

Before I knew it I was naked, lying down with my clothes off under a sheet on the sofa. Of course we had sex, but not just sex, unprotected sex. We both took a major chance: what if he had something, what if I got pregnant? These are the things I think of now but never crossed my mind when I was young, sweet and innocent.

Opening my eyes I looked straight ahead. Chairs, brown table, arms around me. What happened? Turning to the other side of me; I was lying in Sunni's arms. No, no way, we didn't do it, did we? I felt ashamed but deep down I'd enjoyed it. Sunni was fast asleep and I panicked. If someone saw us we were going to be in big trouble. The house was freezing cold, frost blew from my mouth. But all I could think was we need to get up ASAP and get dressed. "Sunni, Sunni!" I softly shouted. "Wake up, wake up."

"What, what?" he said, half asleep, rubbing his eyes trying to figure out where he was.

"You better go upstairs before anyone catches us." Sitting up straight edging his ass off the sofa, standing up, stretching his arms out, tired from the late freaky night before. In a daze staring at this handsome young man I looked at him, he was kind of sexy, very good looking. Was it my lucky day? I never believed I was pretty, I never believed I could ever be loved. He turned around, I was waiting for it.

"I love you," he said as he kissed my forehead then kissed my lips, walking away, shuffling up the stairs on his way to bed. I pulled the sheet over my face in shyness. I could not believe it, someone actually loved me.

The next morning I was unable to look Sunni in the eye feeling shameful, but he treated me like a princess, like I was his world, like I was his woman. I could not understand it so I shied away from Sunni, something I would later regret.

We stayed on the trip for one week and had the best time of our lives, the bonding experience was amazing and I will cherish it forever.

On our last day of the trip we had our last dinner and we spoke of the trip experience. Everyone was excited, for some it was their first time ever being out of London. A few people were open about their experience and about how they felt. I would look at them and think why can't I be like them? Why can't I speak? I had so much to say, so much to express but I was very reserved and watched all the confident people talk while I sat back thinking if I speak will I sound stupid. Eventually I plucked up the courage, or more like Harry kind of forced me. "Right now I'm happy and I want to thank Harry for the experience he has given me." Whoaah thank God for that. Short, sweet and straight to the point. That little speech took my breath away. I was on the verge of shaking from nerves. Everybody clapped with a gleaming smile. I'd done it, I'd faced my fear.

Our last night was very emotional, we all bonded so well and did not want the experience to end. Harry went to the local superstore and purchased some food and we cooked up a storm. To be honest I think we ate spag bol. It was a massive accomplishment; we were so excited we had cooked without any assistance from our parents.

This was the year when Shrek the animated cartoon had come out. Harry bought it on DVD and after dinner we all sat down to watch. Laughing our heads off at the movie, joking around. Tired from the long days prior I could barely keep my eyes open so I headed off to bed saying goodnight to everyone.

Lying in my bed a face appeared beside me. Pretending to be asleep I heard a whisper, "Are you awake?" three times gently bedside my ear. It was Sunni, he had come up the room to see if I was okay.

"Ummm," I replied trying not to move, keeping as still as possible. "Yes what's up?" I said.

"I just wanted to see that you were okay," Sunni replied.

"I'm fine."

He lay beside me, cuddling me, holding me so tight like I've never been held before. Sometimes I close my eyes and think, I wish he could have held me forever and ever and ever. "You know I love you Katrina," he continued to whisper in my ear.

"But you don't know me." How can he love me? There's no way he can love me. I lay in his arms embracing the cuddle, falling into a deep sleep. I will always keep that as a memory; no one has ever held me the same again.

Soon after our return back to London, Sunni took my telephone number. I knew in my heart that I was not going to see Sunni again; I wasn't ready to start a relationship. I wasn't ready to start college, I wanted to party and be free. We all said goodbye to one another and we all went our separate ways. I never returned to the college, I got myself a job at Sunvally Amusements in Harrow. I needed money to fund my lifestyle. Nothing was handed to me in life, I had to fend for myself and by this time I had upgraded from weed and alcohol and started dabbling in cocaine.

I was working but spending as hard as I worked. I became curious about drugs. The white powder was very appealing to me and when I would see people on it having fun talking happily I wanted that feeling. When I would drink and smoke weed I would fall asleep or be very tired, it slowed me down. I wanted to feel that speed that everyone else was feeling. I was going to do it.

I knew a few people who took cocaine and after work I called a guy I knew who sold it and told him to meet me at my mum's. I knew my mum wasn't home so it would be the ideal place, plus I didn't want anyone to know I was taking that stuff. People in my area could chat and believe me that gossip would spread like wildfire. They were obsessed with Katrina Cassandra Newman's life but I didn't know shit about their lives because I was not interested.

When I got home from work it was four in the afternoon, bright and sunny. I made sure my mother wasn't home I made the call. "You got it?"

"Yep see you soon."

"Okie dokey."

He brought this lottery ticket folded all small, and wrapped inside was white powder, a lot of white powder.

"Is this it?"

"Yeah. You sure you want to do this?"

"Yeah I need to stay awake tonight."

"Okay." He was guiding me how to sniff the stuff and said, "Don't do too much, just do enough to make you feel good." He set up two lines on my mum's kitchen table and there we go, one big sniff. I swear we were sniffing for about ten minutes to make sure it all went up our noses. And that was it. I was feeling good, very good.

"Remember," he told me, "the buzz you feel today you will never get again and you're going to chase that buzz."

"Okay," I replied as my cab pulled up ready for me to head out. I don't think I took in what he was really saying to me, I just wanted to feel happy and nice. Little did I know that was an illusion of emotions controlled by a white substance to make you paranoid and crave more. That was something I would later find out in life. Cocaine is a hell of a drug and I'm glad I got myself off it. I could see where it was taking me and it wasn't taking me anywhere good.

I began taking more and more of the cocaine every single day. I was raving more and my confidence boosted beyond measure. I felt unstoppable and believed no one could stop me, or so I thought.

I made a stupid error taking cocaine and this is something I hate. It didn't help with the mental state I was in, I became very aggressive on it but wasn't aware I was. The smallest thing you would say to me would make me snap. I'd go mental and sometimes violent. I started to feel unwell like I was losing myself, just existing but not living. I had a strange kind of feeling but I still managed to get around.

Little did I know, my family was slating me behind my back. The gossip was even travelling to family members who I hadn't seen in years. They didn't even know what I looked like or what I was like. This is where I started to resent the family and get more and more angry. I can't stand two-faced people and gossip, it irritates me beyond belief. Of course people will talk but people should know what to talk about.

Instead of my family trying to help me, they degraded me and to me that's not family. I was calling out for help and no one helped me. The more I heard the angrier I got and my mother made damn sure she would let me know what the family really thought of me.

My attitude towards them was stand-offish and if they came over I would stay in my room. I would mumble to myself, "Two-faced wankers, they better not talk to me," but they would.

"Hi Katrina how are you? How's work?"

"Just fine, work's just fine." And I would leave it at that.

Sunni was ringing my house phone every night but I was never home, I was out partying being the wild child.

One day I was home chilling. Ring, ring the house phone rang. "Hello," I answered.

A deep voice replied, "Hello is Katrina there?"

"Yes it's me who's this?"

"It's Sunni."

I paused. Taking a deep breath I said, "Hiya how's you?" My mum had told me Sunni was calling but I was so wrapped up in my own world I wasn't too bothered.

"What you been up to?" he said. "I've been trying to call you, you're always out."

I chuckled. "Yes I'm always out, I'm young and I'm free."

We talked for a few hours about how much he missed me and wished we could meet up and how he loved spending the week with me, being persistent and not taking no for an answer. I gave in. "Yes okay. I'll come and see you on the weekend."

"I'll ask my mum if you can stay over but you will need to stay in the spare room." "Okay."

"I love you," he replied.

"Okay, see you Saturday." I dropped the phone feeling anxious. What was going on? Why was he so into me? I couldn't understand it, I had no idea what he saw in me, none whatsoever.

I was looking in the mirror, what a mess I looked. It was the Saturday morning, the day I was meeting up with Sunni, the morning after I went out partying on the Friday. Now that the carefree me had to meet a boy who was actually interested in dating me the realisation kicked in: I'd tried to avoid this as much as I could. I wasn't mentally ready for a relationship, no way, no way. I desperately needed a drink; there was no way I could function without it. Running to my local shop I bought a can of K, quickly downing the apple cider. I was trying to see if alcohol was going to make me feel any different, to make me feel more at ease. Nobody understood how I felt or how I functioned. I didn't feel particularly different without the alcohol, but it did calm my nerves.

Ring, ring. On the side of my dressing table my mobile phone started to ring, Sunni flashed up. What do I do? What do I say? I can't, I just can't meet him. I let the phone ring out. He rang again so nervously I answered. "Hi, are you still coming?" he asked.

"Yes, yes, but can we meet in the evening? My mum's asked me to do something for her," I lied. I said it to get out of spending the whole day and night with him.

"Okay make sure you come," he said.

"Yes, yes, I am," I promptly replied.

"Okay see you then. Love you," he always said to me. I could never say that word; I had never known feelings of love.

I wasn't sure what these feelings I was feeling at the time were, but eventually I realised what I was feeling was love. It was pure love. I liked Sunni a lot but not enough for me to let go of my insecurities and let him in to love me. I loved Sunni and he genuinely liked me and I completely messed up something that could have been so nice.

I made my way to Watford to meet Sunni, feeling at ease from the cider I had been drinking throughout the day, gearing myself up to go. I couldn't put this off any longer; if I did he would have given up. I had dissed him long enough. The 142 bus ride was quicker than usual. I got to Watford within thirty minutes; usually it's an hour and a half. I wouldn't have minded stalling that extra hour just to give me a bit more time.

The one thing I was worried about was would he still like me? I don't know why but all kinds of feelings and emotions ran through my mind, like your mind playing tricks on you. I was very careful not to show my angry side, I kept that a secret, but if you spent enough time with me it would eventually come out. Like they say a person cannot hide their true colours for long.

I arrived at Watford station late evening. Standing by the bus doors through the glass I could see a beautiful smile gleaming, there he was waiting for me. I felt so overwhelmed, I felt so happy. All shy-faced I got off the bus trying to control my excitement. He kissed me and hugged me, it felt so right, it felt great. This is where I wanted to be, this was who made me feel happy. Could I make this last forever?

"Hiya," he said, "thank God you're not wearing those slippers." Back then a fashion phase came out Indian slide on slippers and most girls were wearing them. I loved them but sunni could not stand the slippers and he made dam sure he made it clear to me that he did not like my slippers and if he saw me in them I was getting cussed all night long.

I laughed, "Don't worry they're in my bag." He looked at me, shocked. "Only joking I left them at home."

Sunni said he didn't live far from Watford station but boy did he lie, he lived a good forty-five minute walk away. "Do you mind walking? It's a nice evening," he said.

"No not at all," I replied, not knowing what I had geared myself up for. It was the nicest walk I had ever done with him. We laughed and we moaned but most of all we were together.

Arriving at his home all puffed out, he took my coat off as I removed my shoes, a bit apprehensive to meet his family. He turned to me. "Oh by the way my mum and brother have gone on holiday, we have the house to ourselves."

"What?" I replied. "Why didn't you tell me?"

"I didn't think you would come." Shaking my head he led me into the living room. What a beautiful house. It was massive, absolutely massive. Compared to the council home I was raised in this was a palace.

"Would you like a drink?"

"Yes please, what you got?"

"Malibu, brandy, wine…"

"Malibu," I shouted out as he laughed. He placed the drink in my hand and walked over to the TV and turned it on. "Give me a minute I'm going upstairs for a second." "Okay." I sat looking around thinking one day me and Sunni will have kids and have a beautiful house like this far away from all my troubles. I could picture our kids running around the house while I cooked dinner and Sunni lay on the sofa, that would be a dream come true.

A head popped around the corner of the door. "You alright?" It was Sunni asking if I was okay.

"Yes I'm fine, what a lovely house you have."

He walked towards me, putting his hand out. "Come, let's go." I placed my hand into his as we walked towards the bottom of the stairs. I saw candles going up to the top of the stairs on both sides. I looked at Sunni deep into his eyes. This is so sweet I thought. He was really sweet like that, very romantic. It was everything I had ever wanted, everything I had ever dreamed of. He led me up the stairs into the bathroom. I saw the bath was run with candles by the corner of the bath and by the windows and rose petals in the bath. I was actually gobsmacked. It was the first time I actually could not say a word.

He gently took my clothes off. Standing there naked I hated my body, but he loved me, all of me. As he took his clothes off I saw his shyness. He covered his genitals and got in the bath, leading me in after him. The bath was so warm, so romantic. He kissed me. "I love you, are you okay?" This felt like a movie. He was only sixteen, how could he be so sweet? How did he know how to treat me? I didn't have a clue.

He rubbed me down gently, caressing and kissing me all over. For a spilt second I actually thought he saw this in a movie and was practising it on me, it was too good to be true. Gently kissing me as I lay back, his hands were all over my body. "Ummmm I love you," he whispered in my ear. I took a deep breath in but I just couldn't say it. Why I don't know but I felt it, I really felt the love. "I want to make love to you," he said as the water dripped down his face. The eye contact was so deep; it was like our souls catching fire. "Will you be my girlfriend?"

"I want to," I said slowly as my lips locked with his. We kissed so passionately, only stopping to come up for air.

He washed me down and placed the towel around me as I got out the bath. That felt like heaven on earth. I could get used to this treatment. Walking into his bedroom Sunni was kind of hesitant to let me in the room. "What's wrong?"

"Nothing," he replied, "let's get changed downstairs."

"Why?" I said. "What you hiding?" He opened the door. He had a bunk bed. "So what's wrong with that?" I said.

"It's baby. I'm sixteen." I grabbed his face.

"I don't care about that, it doesn't bother me" That made Sunni feel so at ease his whole mannerism changed to an overwhelming happy feeling. We got changed into our night clothes and went into the guest room. The guest room was beside the conservatory just before the back garden. It had a TV, was full of books and had a small bathroom and a sofa bed.

Sunni pulled the sofa bed out and fluffed the pillows, spread out the quilts and we got ready to lie down, drinking and smoking. We talked, laughed, joked. He got upset with me because I was not so open. I would always listen to him but never talk about me. I didn't have anything to say; I had never been on holiday, I had never been taken anywhere nice as I got older. Talking about Devon when you were about eight years old when Sunni was talking about going to Spain, America, Australia; I couldn't even compare my life to that. All I did was party and get drunk. As Sunni told me stories I would wonder how nice that must feel, on holiday with his mum, dad brother and family.

That was very much alien to me. My mother never took me anywhere and my father took everyone else everywhere and supported everyone else apart from me. There's not one picture with me and my mother and that speaks volumes in itself: selfish. Her life was all about how she suffered and how her life was bad. I always think why did she have children?

Sunni would tell me beautiful stories about his family but also he had it hard and was struggling when his father left the family home to set up a new life with his new family. Sunni really struggled with that. When he would speak of his dad he would get so angry but when he spoke of his mum he was so happy. I knew there was an issue there and I knew something was up. Eventually he opened up and explained why he was feeling that way. I don't want to say what his problem was as it's his personal business and this is my book so I will keep that part out of it. But I can say even though he was fighting a battle no one knew about he was still a sweetie, and was very sweet to me, even though he could be an asshole sometimes like most boys.

The good talk we had that night was amazing. He trusted me and felt comfortable enough to tell me how he felt. I will forever cherish that moment. There are moments in life that just stick with you and that's one of them.

We were both high and very merry from the Malibu. As he edged himself off the bed, BANG! I heard.

"What's that?"

As I sat up, "Arrrrggghhh!" he groaned. "I just knocked your drink over. That was your fault."

"No it's not."

"Yes it is."

"How?"

"If you had drunk your bloody drink." "Don't bloody speak to me like that," I replied sternly.

He giggled, "I'm sorry." He cleaned up the spilt drink and jumped back into the bed. He turned the TV off keeping the side lamp on.

"Can you see me?" I laughed, making a joke that I was black in the dark.

"Of course. Why are you being so stupid? You're not even black, you're brown," he said jokingly, leaning in for a kiss. He kissed me and all my worries and hurt feelings faded away. I felt protected, loved and happy.

That was the first and only time in all my life. I have never had that feeling again, no one can touch me the same, no one can make me feel that feeling and I ask myself why? Our little fondle when we went away with the group from our college did not count, this was me and him alone and how he made me feel wonder. I'm jealous that he will be giving another girl the love he gave me and more, I feel he should have been mine. I should have fought harder for him. I should have told him how I really felt and I'm sorry for this, I really am.

I felt goosebumps on my arms; I felt the sweet, tender kiss on my lips. Cupid struck my heart and that very moment I knew I never wanted to be apart from him. I felt my heart skip a beat, I felt the heavens open. When he looked into my eyes I knew that he was a beautiful gift. When he held my hand and caressed my face I knew that very moment I was in love with him and he loved me. I had finally found what I was looking for: love.

That night we made love, it was the best feeling I had ever felt. It wasn't just a feeling, we made life.

I woke up the next morning in his arms. "Good morning." Sunni was already up but didn't want to wake me up

"How long have you been awake?" I said as I rubbed my eyes.

"A little while, I didn't want to wake you up." Rolling out of bed, he said, "You hungry babe? I make a mean breakfast." That was his favorite word, mean, everything was mean.

Getting up to shower I made my way upstairs. The candles must have burnt out themselves; I think we were too drunk to remember to put them out. Thank God the house didn't go up in flames.

I had work later that afternoon so I needed to leave by 12pm because I started work at 1pm. We cuddled on the sofa, chilling and reminiscing about the night before. Before I knew it, it was twelve and my taxi was there. Sunni picked up my bag and escorted me to the cab, putting my bag down on the back seat. I sat beside my bag. He leaned in and kissed me goodbye. "I'll call you later."

"Okay."

"I love you."

I smiled, embracing the moment. My heart felt love but my mouth couldn't say it. What a fool, what a fool I was.

It was a beautiful Sunday and I'd had a beautiful night in high spirits. I went to work so happy, so vibrant, and so excited; no one could disturb my peace. While in the cab Sunni called me, he was very caring, very loving, speaking of the night before. He was very respectful and showed how much he cared. I spoke to him until I got to work which wasn't too far from his house. "Bye babe have a good day, I'll speak to you later, love you."

"Bye speak to you later."

For once in my life I knew I could make this different. I knew I could have a happy future, a happy life.

I was at work for a couple of hours. I was supposed to finish at 10pm, but my back started to hurt and I could barely stand up. "Lisa look at my back it's killing me." I slowly took my top off and she gasped, "Your back is bruised, what happened to you?"

"Nothing, I must have fallen." I kept Sunni a secret for a bit; he was my little bit of pleasure. I didn't want my mother to find out I was dating Sunni and if I'd told Lisa she would have told my mum. I knew how I got the bruises and couldn't believe that a bath could cause that much damage. I was sent home to rest, too unwell to work. I took a cab home and went straight to bed.

Waking up later that evening, I saw a few missed calls and texts from friends, Lisa, and Sunni. I must have been so tired from the night before, when I hit that bed I made up for loss of sleep.

Sitting up in bed I thought about last night's event. Still very smitten I called Sunni back.

"Hello," he said, "where you been I called your work."

"I was sent home, my back is bruised." "What happened?"

"I think I bruised it in the bath."

He laughed, "Oh yes, oh." I could picture his cheeky smile as he was saying it.

"You meeting me tonight?"

"Not tonight I've got work at six in the morning."

"Okay I will see you at the weekend."

"Okay, love you, bye."

The following week was a chill-out week – work, life, work mode. Me and Sunni corresponded by phone throughout the week. He was working, I was working and we had no time to see one another. The weekend was fast approaching and I was feeling tired, more tired than usual. Sunni wanted to meet up on the weekend. I really couldn't be bothered to but I told him I was coming down. This is where our relationship started to become awkward. I promised to meet Sunni and Ryan down Harrow and we would go up to his house that weekend. I never turned up; no explanation, no phone calls. I went out partying instead. I was really selfish and I thought I could treat people this way and it was okay. I believed they would never leave me. Boy did I get the shock of my life.

Ryan and me were friends from Willesden College we studied performing arts together. I was really shocked to see Ryan on the same course in Watford a couple of years later. We clicked straight away and he remembered who I was from college. We built up a really good relationship, but it was the four of us: me, Sunni, Ryan and Billy who was really close by in college. Billy never came out much but we would go to his dorm and watch TV, drink, smoke and talk about all kinds of shit.

Looking down at my phone constantly ringing, Sunni's number flashed before me. I can't tell you why but I just was not interested in meeting him that weekend. I wanted to party, I wanted to go out with my friends. That was more important, that was priority. I went out and partied the night away letting my phone ring out all night. Now thinking about it I was a bitch towards Sunni I and regret treating him that way.

THE LOVE OF A MOTHER

I woke up the next morning all hung over. I rolled over, squinting at my phone: messages and missed calls. I called Sunni but the phone rang out. I called his house phone. "Hello," a soft gentle voice answered.

"Hello," I said, "is Sunni there?"

"Oh hi, are you Katrina?" Now I had clocked it was Sunni's mum. "I've heard so much about you, but I want to say Sunni has a phone bill for £200 talking to you for hours throughout the day and night."

"Oh sorry," I said.

"No it's not your fault," Sunni's mum replied. "He was stating he didn't know whose number this was." I chuckled. "Nice talking to you, hope to see you soon."

"Yes sure, same."

A deep voice came on the phone. "Hiya, why did you call the house phone?" he said in a soft voice.

"Because you're not answering your mobile phone."

"I lost it last night. Where were you?"

"Sorry," I said, "I wasn't feeling too well." "Why didn't you call me to come down and be with you?"

"Oh sorry, I slept right through." A lie that would eventually catch up to me.

"You coming to see me today?"

"Sorry I can't I'm working, but I will come and see you soon."

That week was so stressful at work but I managed to party throughout the week, hung over most days but mastering my work like the back of my hand. Not even a pounding headache could stop my flow. Sunni met me from work on the Friday. It was such a beautiful summer's day and I had worked the morning shift. Sunni had also finished work early so we had the rest of the day to ourselves.

Throughout my whole life, as messed up as my mother was, she never ever taught me about people's colour, not even my own. This was the first day I felt racism and it was very strange to me. We got on the train at Harrow station. While we were at the station Sunni was asking for a kiss. Seeing everyone staring at us I rejected him. He looked at me in utter shock wondering what was wrong with me shying away. I didn't know why the people on the platform were looking at us. We got on the train and headed towards Watford station. That day I started to feel strange like is this for me? Why can't I show affection? Why do I feel strange to show love? I love him I know I do but why can't I tell him? We got off at Watford station. It was a bright lovely afternoon, everyone around walking, shopping, enjoying the sun. Walking out of the station he held my hand. I smiled thinking yes, I think this is right. As I turned to my left I saw a couple overtly staring. The lady was pointing us out to her husband, I'm assuming she said, "Look, look at those two." It was not a good look on the woman's face; she looked at Sunni and me in disgust.

Sunni saw her vague but nasty look. "Fuck off! Fuck 'em, don't worry, and ignore them." I let his hand go, and from that day I decided I no longer felt comfy dating a white boy.

I should have actually said fuck them, he's the boy I love and want to grow old with and give it a chance. But my feelings got the better of me and I messed around the one person who actually cared for me.

He stopped and reassured me it was okay and he loved me no matter what. We walked to the Harlequin in the city centre of Watford where we met Abdi. Abdi was a friend of ours from the YMCA course. We all became good friends and spent a lot of time together. Abdi was born in Somalia and settled in Watford with his family, a troubled boy just like the rest of us. Abdi sold weed at the time and Sunni used to pick up his weed from him, so Sunni called Abdi to pick up some weed. Once we collected it we then headed straight to Sunni's home. Once again we were home alone, Sunni's mum was away for the night. Chilling out for the rest of the day drinking and smoking we chose not to go out and stayed home. We actually liked each other's company. I would moan about him, he would moan about me but we would laugh it off most of the time. Lying in his arms that night I felt a sense of warmness, calmness, and happiness. The way the old couple looked at me and Sunni crossed my mind while lying in his arms, looking down at his hands on my side. They had looked at us in disgust. I was really shocked. It was something

I had never seen before, something I had never experienced. Everyone experiences racism and I can tell you one thing for sure, I did not like it one bit.

The next day at work I was thinking about the facts of the day before and really disliked it. I didn't think about leaving Sunni, that happened all by itself due to my actions. I blame myself for not speaking out and telling him how I really felt. I think about my life and how it could have been, how it should have been, and if I had done things better maybe my life wouldn't have been so dramatic, but when you've been let down all your life you kind of expect the dramatic lifestyle.

That day work was an eventful one. We were joking around and I couldn't wait to go out that night with my friends. This was when I started to become distant from Sunni but was still very close to Ryan. Me and Ryan talked on the phone most days and met up. I actually met up with Ryan more than I did with Sunni, how strange, but I got on better with Ryan. Having a male friend that I could tell everything to and it goes no further is like a dream come true for a girl. Well, I thought he kept all my secrets. A few he let loose as I found out later on.

After work we partied so hard, it's like I missed the wild me. Sunni kind of had me controlled to a degree, I acted like the perfect girlfriend. He never knew I took cocaine, I kept that away from him, but he knew I smoked weed and drank alcohol. I kept a lot swept under the carpet when it came to Sunni. I just wished he would say to me, "It's going to be okay, I see your pain," but I guess he was going through his own trials and tribulations, and we were both young trying to find ourselves in life.

I started to meet up with Ryan and Billy and when Sunni was coming from work or was popping over to Billy's I would go home. I avoided all of Sunni's phone calls and went out with my friends.

One day I answered. "I heard you came down."

"Yes only for a bit."

"Why didn't you wait for me?"

"Sorry I had to go home."

"Okay when I can see you?"

"The weekend, I'm working all week."

"Okay. I've missed you." He always had the right talk at the right time, but I was so far gone and my home life was terrible to live in. I could never date Sunni and have the perfect future, my mother would destroy it or I would so I stayed away.

I headed on holiday to Jamaica so that gave us time apart and my feelings for Sunni started to fade.

My brother Leonardo paid for me to go to Jamaica, it was my first trip overseas. I have always been grateful for this. He took me for my eighteenth birthday and I was supposed to have spent it there but the plans changed. I became very sick within the weeks I spent out there and was unable to enjoy my holiday. I spent most of my time in bed and a private doctor came out to assess me, thinking that drinking the tap water had given me a bug, but it was no bug I had caught. Throughout my trip I was constantly poorly and vomiting. The heatstroke was killing me and for once I just wanted to go home. I could barely stand up, my legs and arms were skinny but my boobs and tummy were not going down and from all the vomiting you would think I would be skinny as hell, unable to eat anything.

It was lovely seeing my family and it was lovely seeing Jamaica but I just couldn't hack it anymore so I got the first flight back to London just before my eighteenth birthday. I was supposed to be out in Jamaica loving the sun for two months but I lasted two weeks. Sometimes I wished I had stayed, but some things are just not meant to be.

Returning back to London, I felt a bit better, not 100% but better than I did. I got back to working and meeting friends. Sunni was not on my mind but I let him know I was back in London. He was actually happy to hear from me. I was very surprised he had missed me.

I woke up early one morning for work as my alarm went off. I was getting hardly any sleep from feeling so rough, I was feeling very unwell. I just put it down to going out and working too hard, but I hadn't felt great going out and wasn't able to drink my drinks, leaving the clubs stone-cold sober, just wanting my bed.

Sitting on the edge of my bed a full force of sickness filled my mouth. I clutched my mouth running to the toilet. Before I could reach the seat, vomit hit the closed lid, splashing back at me and against the walls. I was still trying to lift the toilet seat hoping some would go into the toilet. After I had sprayed the whole toilet with vomit I breathed with relief, gasping for breath. I stretched my head back, looking down at this toilet. How the hell was I going to clean this up feeling so sick? I must still have that bug from Jamaica!

Heading to work I felt like utter shit but I had to work. That day I worked but not with any force in me. I was vomiting for the whole day. I just couldn't wait to get home. I didn't want to speak to anyone, so I was very quiet on my shift. My co-worker Lilly asked me if I was okay. I sat in the staffroom and jumped out the chair and ran to the toilet. The sounds of me vomiting echoed through the shop floor and staffroom. Knock knock. "Katrina are you okay?"

"Yes yes," I tried to reply, stepping out a few minutes later wiping my mouth with the tissue.

"Come back into the staffroom," Lilly asked me "Katrina you don't have to tell me but are you pregnant?" I looked at her like how can I be pregnant? You must be mad. To be honest I was none the wiser about what was happening, I still thought I had a bug. "Listen," she told me, "I know those symptoms and it is pregnancy. Go get yourself checked out." Unable to answer I nodded, letting Lilly know I would go to the GP and get checked over. She was holding me really tight, I think she felt sorry for me. The one thing I rate Lilly for is that she never told a soul about my pregnancy and I wondered how she knew.

Returning from work late that evening, all worked out and tired as hell, all I wanted to do was have a bath and sleep, but my house was full of family. My cousin Syreeta and other relatives were drinking and Mother was smoking weed. I greeted everyone and slowly dragged myself upstairs. I lay flat on my bed, clothes and shoes on, closing my eyes ready to sleep but itching to have a bath that would give me the sleep that I needed, that relaxing sleep. Sensing something above me I opened my eyes halfway. Syreeta was standing over me as I lay like a starfish. She was talking to me but I could hardly understand her, I was half asleep. "What did you say?"

"Look at the size of your boobs."

I stood up looking in the mirror as she stood beside me. "Are you pregnant?"

"No," I said in my defense.

"By whom? That guy you're seeing, what's his name again?"

"No, no, I haven't seen him for a while." Looking down at my chest my breasts were kind of large, but I still was none the wiser.

I ran a nice hot bubble bath, I couldn't wait to get in and relax. I was thinking about what Lilly and Syreeta said. Can I be? How? What if I am? What am I going to do? I decided the next morning I would book a doctor's appointment just to make sure I wasn't, but it really started to make me think. I hadn't had a period in two months.

That evening I was so tired I jumped into bed and fell straight asleep with no worries on my mind. I actually got a good night's sleep. No drama, no headache.

The next morning first thing I called the GP. I was off work that day which I was grateful for; I could get some rest. The GP gave me a morning appointment and I think my mother knew something wasn't right, she wasn't abusing me as much and was very calm. She had heard my conversation with the GP over the phone and insisted on coming with me. Sitting waiting for my turn they called me. My mother stood up but I told her, "No, this is private." You could see she was vexed but what could she do? I was eighteen now and did not need aid or assistance for anything. I was now officially an adult.

"What can I do for you Katrina?"

"Well I've been sick for some time. I went to Jamaica, they said I caught a bug but it's not going away." Dr Stein looked at me, it was the funniest look.

"A bug. Ah, so are you sexually active?" she asked.

"Yes."

"When was your last period?"

"Two months ago."

"Go and take this test tube. Wee into it and come back." I was very anxious but still convinced it was a bug. I weed into the test tube and returned back to the room. Placing her gloves on Dr Stein opened the lid of the test tube and placed a stick inside which had a measuring meter. I sat there looking at her waiting on the result. Sitting back into her chair she said, "Katrina, you are pregnant!" If the floor could have opened and taken me away there and then I wouldn't have minded.

"WHAT!"

"Yes, you're pregnant and I'm guessing you're two and a half months gone. What would you like to do?"

"I'm not keeping it, no I can't. My mum's going to kill me."

"Well I will send you for a scan, you have three weeks to decide."

In utter shock I wanted to cry but the tears wouldn't come out of my eyes. How on earth could I sort this? How the hell did this happen? I felt more fucked than I did before. As I walked out the room Dr Stein said, "Take care of yourself Katrina." I think my face said it all.

"What did she say?" asked my mother.

"Nothing, I've got a bug."

And I walked straight out the GP not knowing what the fuck to do.

The next couple of days I worked and stayed home, not telling anyone a thing, but I had a feeling they knew. At some point I needed to call Sunni and tell him. How could I tell him this? I'd been so horrible to him but I had to tell him at some point, he had a right to know. So I called Sunni to meet up, which he was happy to do. Yet again we stayed at his house. I was very quiet and thinking how can I drop this bomb? So I played box clever asking him questions about kids. "Do you want kids?"

"Yes of course but not now."

"How many do you want?"

"Two."

"What if I got pregnant?"

"I would support you but I'm too young to be a dad, I want to travel you know, live life before that."

I felt my world just crash before me. There was no way I was telling him I was pregnant, no way. I was so upset but he never knew what I was thinking, that I was carrying his child. The way I handled things was very silly, I would test the situation to see how you responded and then I would judge you, like I wanted to know how loyal you were. I was so upset that Sunni wanted a life and I was there pregnant so I started an argument. "When are you going to grow up? All you do is rave, drink and smoke." I turned nasty, a side he had never seen in me before.

"What? It's my life and you're not my mum. No one is going to make me change."

That was it, I had made my mind up and as soon as I got back to London I was going to do what I needed to do.

That day was very bitter between Sunni and me and that was the last day I saw him for a long time, I had completely written him off. I was stubborn and foolish. Sunni tried to call me on many occasions but I ignored his calls. He came to my work but I was just distant.

One day I met up with Ryan. He knew what had happened between me and Sunni and he was worried if Sunni knew he was with me. "Why?"

"I don't know we were friends first."

My mum had gone away with a guy she was seeing and Ryan stayed over at mine. We went for a few drinks and went home. That evening I told him I was pregnant. He asked if it was Sunni's. "Yes," I said, "but don't tell him." I didn't want Ryan going back and telling Sunni I was pregnant, it would mess everything up. I had told Ryan secrets before and he'd never told a soul.

"I'm not keeping it," I told him.

"Why?"

"Nah, I'm too young and that's why I don't want you to tell Sunni." I thought my secret was safe with Ryan but I guess it clearly wasn't. I still hadn't contacted Sunni and Sunni did not contact me. I was keeping my distance.

I went for my three-month scan at the Royal Free Hospital alone, I had no feelings whatsoever, I just felt numb. Waiting to be seen I looked around, wondering, sitting, and waiting for my turn to be called in for the scan. "Katrina?" a voice called from the room in front.

"Yes." Feeling startled they'd called me.

"Hi my lovely. So you're going to be scanned today but because you're not keeping the baby you need to look away."

"Okay," I replied feeling anxious, but keeping it cool.

"Can you lie this way for me please?" the nurse said. Placing myself down on to the bed I pulled my top to the top of my tummy and my trousers low. The lady covered me with a blanket and put the gel on my tummy. "You ready?" she said, smiling at me. "This is going to be a bit cold."

"Okay," I replied looking down at the bottom of the bed feeling shame that I was there. All I was thinking at this point was that she must be thinking something bad. I was a young girl having a termination, this must be awful.

"I'm going to turn the screen away."

As she placed the ultrasound on to my tummy I heard the heartbeat. From the corner of my eye I could see on the screen a small baby, very tiny, moving around. I smiled. "Is the baby okay?"

"I can't tell you my love, unless you're keeping the baby."

"I just want to know."

She looked at me. "The baby's okay."

"What's the sex?"

"It's best you don't ask Hun if you're not keeping the baby and at this stage we don't know."

I was happy for a second. I had the power to bring life into the world. I saw my child on the screen. That was my child, God gave me a gift. I really needed to think about this, this was my last chance. After this my appointment would be booked and that would be it.

Leaving the hospital, unsure what I was going to do, I was more confused than when I went in. But the image of my child moving around on the screen will forever stay with me forever.

I ended up becoming really sick. I couldn't work and was constantly vomiting and was very dehydrated. I had my appointment at the Royal Free Hospital and my mum was waiting until that date to take me in. I was unable to walk and my mum made me take the train. I could hardly stand up. As I got through the doors I collapsed. I was quite happy collapsing there as I was in good hands. They rushed me onto a ward. "She's pregnant," I heard faintly. "Get this girl on a drip, now."

I heard the doctor telling my mum, "Why didn't you bring her in sooner? She could have died." My mother was implying she didn't think I was that unwell. "Tut tut," the doctor said. "Look at her, does she look well?"

They placed me on a drip and told me to get some rest. My mother bent her head down in shame as they took care of me. In and out of sleep I started to feel so much better. I thanked the doctors. "Thank you."

"How are you feeling?"

"Better, much better."

"Good, good. You will be here for a few days but tomorrow we will talk to you about…" and he paused. I was assuming the baby.

"Okay," I said and lay back down, looking at him as he walked off. This was my last chance to make it right, don't be scared, try and be a good mum, try and make it work. But I just couldn't and that morning I had made my mind up; I was having a termination. Nothing and no one was going to stop me. When my mum found out the look of relief on her face, thinking about it now, it was definitely a happy face, a face of joy and relief that I was not going to have the baby.

If I'd had the child I would be gone, living my life with my family and there would be no one to blame and no one to abuse. She was actually scared for once, scared I would have a life and be happy and she would be alone, all alone.

My mother controlled her surroundings when it came to me. Telling lies, stealing, you name it she'd done it and blamed me for all her shenanigans and people actually believed her. My mother could and can manipulate a situation and if you don't know her you will believe her, she's that good. She could have put her talent to work, she should have become a lawyer she's that good at convincing someone that you're in the wrong. When I told my mother I was pregnant I knew she knew. She never said a word to me; she was quiet, very quiet.

It doesn't come with a rulebook, how you are going to feel after you have a termination. Yes you get a booklet but there was no counselling, there was no emotional support, nothing. Just go home and deal with it. Coming from a dysfunctional home it was not the ideal place for me to be, back into toxic surroundings full of emotional and unstable energy. It was not good, not good at all. It just made me ten times worse with all the emotions I was feeling running around my poor little head. I didn't know who to turn to or how to deal with it. It was one of the worst feelings I have ever felt in my life. At the tender age of eighteen I was lost. This affected my whole life, my whole well-being, including how I saw myself and how I saw other people.

After the termination I was in hospital for a week and then returned home. The hospital and the staff were really nice to me and looked after me really well. Coming home felt very strange. I wanted to change my career path. I wanted to become a nurse. I'm not sure why but I love helping people, it gives me a great pleasure. Maybe it's because I was never given a silver spoon growing up, so looking out for those who are in need and need love gave me a good feeling.

My household was good and peaceful for at least a week or two, and then the madness began again. My mother was drinking, taking drugs, smoking, bursting into my room at 3am abusing me: "Do the dishes!" Now I had nowhere to run to, I had to stay home and face the abuse. In a deep sleep I would get woken up to screaming in my face. "You bitch, why didn't you wash the dishes? You whore, you slut, you tramp," her trademark abusive words. It was a regular routine. Oh yes after the termination I was called every degrading name under the sun. You name it she said it to me after 3am. By 4/5am she would be so fucked she would pass out on the sofa. Lights on, TV on, bottles of vodka, weed everywhere, house a shithole, and I would always get the blame. I was already going through my mental state of what I had just been through; there was no way I could deal with her shit, no way. It was way too much to handle. I know Sunni could have saved me.

Calling Sunni I told him I needed him but he had moved on, partying and meeting other girls. He started to be very distant and was talking to me but didn't want to meet up. I really needed him but he was so blank to me. I was completely lost. We would talk on the phone for hours but he wouldn't meet me or tell me to come up. I was thinking something was really strange.

I kept in contact with Ryan a lot and we decided to meet up. My mother had met a guy from Ghana and was seeing him, he had taken her on holiday to Germany and I had the house to myself so I invited Ryan to stay over for the weekend. We chilled, went for a few drinks up the pub and I started to get drunk. I hadn't had a drink in a while and I got drunk, quite an emotional wreck. I blurted out, "I had the abortion."

"What?"

"I had the abortion," toning down my voice.

"What, Sunni's baby?"

"Yes, yes," feeling like a fool and knowing he would tell Sunni what I'd said.

"Oh my god are you all right?"

"Yeah, yeah. I'm fine." But I wasn't fine at all I just wanted someone to save me.

But I didn't get saved, all that happened was Ryan told Sunni that I'd aborted his child. The next time me and Sunni spoke it was not on good terms and that's when I knew I had messed up everything. He never directly told me he knew but I knew from when Ryan left me to me speaking to Sunni that something was said. The last words I remember Sunni saying to me over the phone were, "You bitch." I replied that yes I was a bitch but not by choice. Sunni has never forgiven me for this; I guess I understand his pain.

I became out of control completely gone mentally. I didn't know myself at all. I was taking hard drugs regularly; I didn't care about life. I didn't care about myself at this point, fuck it what have I got to lose? What have I got to live for? Partying, drinking, and being carefree.

Three months on back at work I met a guy called Ricki, he worked with my cousin Syreeta at Ladbrokes in Harrow.

One day I was chilling at my cousin's house and she was talking about a young mixed-race guy at her work. "The kind of guys Katrina likes."

"What?" I replied. "Yeah you like mixed-race kind of guys.

I laughed, "Let me see him," so she called him and we spoke on the phone briefly. I was none the wiser about this guy, he was just another guy in London to be honest. I was doing so much coke that I most probably met him because I was just high as fuck and wanted a link to heal my sore wounds.

We spoke a few times on the phone and arranged to meet up. He came down to me and we chilled for a bit. My mother left the house and went to visit a friend, so we were home alone. He had weed and drinks and I was taking coke.

There is nothing romantic about the next bit, he was very polite and was very shy.

We began to kiss, lying down on my bed fully clothed. He tried to push his penis in. "Wait!" I shouted. "You got any condoms?" "Na, na but I'll pull out don't worry, I know what I'm doing." I took his word for it. He pulled up my skirt, slowly kissing and caressing my neck, using his hand to find the entry. As Ricki lay on top of me he froze.

"You alright?" I said as I looked to the side, trying to look to see if he was okay.

Faintly he replied, "I've cum."

"WHAT! No way? How?"

"Yeah I did."

I was so shocked. I looked down; I was as dry as a whistle. I was still baffled if he did or he didn't. "Okay." I took his word for it, I just thought he was drunk and he couldn't perform.

He got up, holding his head in shame. "I'm drunk, I'm so sorry I really am. It must be the beers."

"It's okay, it's cool, don't worry about it."

Ricki went home feeling shamed that night, apologising to me on the telephone all the way home as he travelled on the 183 back to Pinner. I couldn't even laugh it felt so surreal. So, as you do, I set up a line of coke, couple of swigs of Jack and off I went to the Pochines to party the night away. I wasn't wasting my night for anyone and it was only 11pm.

I was not feeling Ricki at all and he was not feeling me, but we still spoke via the phone now and again joking about the madness that had happened, but I was very distant. To be honest I don't think I was feeling anyone at that time; I just wanted to be alone.

Two months later I was getting on with my life: working, partying, trying to get by and be happy. My period was nowhere to be seen and I became unwell, being sick, you know, bug-like symptoms but this time I was fully aware as to what my symptoms were. The same symptoms as before and I knew straight away. I just wanted confirmation and if I was how the fuck was I going to explain this one? I was already being called every single hurtful, hateful name, what would she call me now? What was my family going to think of me? I knew my mother would not keep any of my personal affairs a secret; the more she could tarnish me the better.

I headed to my local Sainsbury's. I didn't have any money on me. Yet again I was all alone dealing with this situation, standing in aisle 13 staring at the pregnancy tests. There were so many, which one do I buy? Not only can I not buy this item, but how can I leave without getting caught? I grabbed the pregnancy test and ran out of Sainsbury's all the way home. I didn't stop till I reached my front door all puffed out.

I quickly went upstairs and opened the test real quick, reading the instructions. Wee on the stick for a couple of seconds and wait two minutes. Two lines means you're pregnant, one line means you're not. I rushed to the toilet and weed on the stick straight away. It was like the wee was waiting for the stick. Sitting on the toilet waiting, trousers still down, tapping my leg. Two minutes were up. I turned the stick over.

Two thick pink lines appeared. This could not be happening, no fucking way, not to me how the fuck could this happen? This time I was angry. I was so angry with myself; I was pregnant by a guy I hardly even fucking knew, what a piss-take, what a slap in the face. Three months prior I had just aborted Sunni's baby. How could I ever look my family in the face?

This was too good to be true. I went back to see Dr Stein all ashamed in sin. "I think I'm pregnant." The look Dr Stein gave me, I said to myself she must think I'm absolutely disgusting. Barely opening my mouth I hardly spoke a word in the doctor's room.

"Well you know what to do." She handed me the glass tube and off I went to the toilet to wee into it, still wishing and hoping it would come back negative. I went back into the room; the wee filled the tube to the top, dark yellow. My wee did not look healthy and I did feel like shit, sitting anxious waiting for the results. Thinking about all kinds of things I went into deep thinking. As an echo I heard, "Positive." Was I dreaming? The echo started to fade as I came out from my daydream. "Yes Katrina, you're pregnant again." If the floor could open and me just drop into it and seal me up I would have been so happy.

"Fuck." I put my hands on my face. "Not again, no way. How the fuck could I be?" It was impossible.

"So Katrina what are you planning to do?"

Life could not get any worse than what I was facing but it just did. I left the doctor's more upset than I ever was before. Feeling sad I just went home and lay in bed thinking about what I was going to do next. The one thing I knew was this time I was going to do the right thing, I was going to tell Ricki I was pregnant. However he responded to it I would just deal with it, like most of the things in my life I dealt with. But for now I just wanted to rest so I slept.

The next morning I was feeling so rough. The sun was shining through my curtains and my room was so hot. I just wanted air. I got out of bed and opened the window. The smell from the fresh breeze and the green grass was so nice. Heading downstairs I got myself a glass of water, and headed back upstairs. Looking at my phone I saw loads of missed calls, a few people but mostly from Ricki. Right then I couldn't deal with talking to him. I flipped the phone over and jumped back into bed. Lying on my back I noticed the house was ever so quiet. My mum was not home. Yes, peace, I finally got some peace.

I had to go back to the hospital for a check up. This time I wasn't too sure if I should keep the baby but I knew it would be very difficult if I did. I never knew Ricki, we had only met twice, once for a drink and dinner and the next well you know what happened there. How could I raise a child with a man I hardly knew? I had a few weeks to decide what I was going to do but in the meantime I was brave enough to tell my mother I was pregnant again and she was not impressed. All her face showed was anger. Again she didn't say a word to me. She kept her cool and I wasn't fazed if she cared or not. I just thought what am I going to do?

I actually thought this could be my ticket out, a council flat with my baby and me. But no father? I didn't want my child to be raised like me, fatherless. Could this work between me and Ricki? I was really thinking is this my time to be a mother? My head was all over the place, but while I was confused Ricki was looking out for me asking was I okay. He wanted to see me and look after me, and said whatever I did he would support me. I thought that was really nice but I did not want to give Ricki mixed signals. I didn't want to lead him on. If I was going to make up my mind and not have the baby I would feel very bad doing that to him. Deep inside I was wishing something good would come out of this but I can be so stubborn, something I have worked on over the years. I don't like to be hurt so if I can avoid you or hurt you first it would make me feel a little bit better, but not really. It was a mask I was portraying to hide my insecurities. I never thought anyone would really love or like me. And I never thought I had so much love in me to give to someone else. I was scared, scared shitless.

My appointment came and I had to attend the Royal Free Hospital. Ricki was adamant he wanted to come to the hospital with me but I could see where this was heading and I said no. He kept going on and on, "Let me be there with you, I'll take the day off work."

"NO!" I replied. I didn't feel it was good for him to attend the scan; it would bring up all kind of emotions so I went alone.

"Call me when you get back."

"Okay," I said and went on my journey, now thinking of it I really needed someone there, I needed help and support but didn't know how to ask for it. I was used to dealing with things myself so it felt normal.

"Katrina." The nurse called me in to the scanning room. "Hi." The nurse introduced herself and asked if I was okay.

"Yes," I replied but deep inside I wasn't ready, nor was I alright. But I put my brave smiley face on and was ready to do what I had to do.

Asking my name and date of birth the nurse asked me to proceed with lying on the bed and pulling my top up to my chest and my trousers just below my waist and she placed a blanket for my dignity to cover up my private area. Pulling the screen away from me she asked me not to look at the screen but I wanted to and from the glimpse I got I saw a baby on the screen, a small, tiny little baby. I asked the nurse, "Is the baby okay?"

She replied, "Are you keeping the baby?"

I muttered, "No," but really wanted to say yes.

"Well I can't tell you and it's best you don't know."

"Please," I said, "I'm okay. I just want to know the baby's okay.

Looking at me she said, "Do you really want to know? This is not going to be easy." I looked directly into her eyes. "Okay then, the baby's fine," she quickly told me and continued to finish up the scan in a weird way. I felt happy that nothing was wrong with my baby. Maybe if there was something wrong it would make my choice so much easier, but the choice was harder and harder and harder to make.

I returned home feeling like shit, and more confused. Seeing my baby made it feel more real that there was a life growing inside of me and it was up to me to bring forth this life into the world. I had many missed calls from Ricki, but I wasn't in the mood to talk to him, I wasn't in the mood to talk to anyone. It was draining, tiring a hard day, mentally and emotionally, so I went to bed hoping I would feel much better in the morning.

The next morning arrived and I actually got a good nights sleep. Maybe I needed it but I didn't feel better, but life must go on and I had to go to work. The house was quiet and for once there was no trouble. It looked like when I was pregnant my mother left me alone. Kind of strange, but she never abused or troubled me when I was pregnant, she just never spoke to me which I was happy with because she never said anything nice to me so it was a win-win situation.

I was very quiet at work just getting on with my job. Ricki was trying his best to get in contact with me but I wasn't in the mood to talk to anyone. I was kind of fed up and when I'm like that I just stay quiet. I really had nothing to say. Work was running slow. I kept watching the clock, waiting for 2pm so I could go home and rest. Work started to become long for me so I took some time off work to get myself together. My manager was Lisa, she got me the time I needed. I just needed time to clear my head so I took two weeks off and it was well needed.

Yet again my appointment was due for my termination. I had told Ricki the date, time and location. He was willing to support me but I was not having any of it, I just didn't want him around me. But we did speak on the phone a few times. I became more distant, in my own shell, and knew once this termination was done I would block off all contact with him.

The Royal Free Hospital was three miles away from my home; it was very easy for me to commute. One straight train and a little walk to the hospital from Belize Park station. Going there I didn't feel anything, no fear, no pain, no sadness. Emotionless.

Yet again I was in familiar circumstances but this time I was in a cubicle and had to wait with other girls and ladies who were also having a termination. That made me feel a little bit at ease knowing I wasn't the only one going through this horrible affair. I seem to get really good nurses when I'm in hospital. The nurse who attended to me was really nice, polite and sympathetic, reassuring me that I was going to be okay and making sure this was what I wanted, that I was ready to go ahead with the procedure.

Ricki called once I had finished with the nurse. "Are you okay?" he asked.

"Yes I'm fine."

"You sure you don't want me to come?" he asked.

"No, why would you? It's not nice to see."

"I just want to support you and be there for you."

"No I'm okay. I'm going to go now, speak to you after."

"Okay."

Come to think of it he really wanted to support me and be that gentleman I needed. He wasn't going to allow me to do this alone but my stubbornness would not let him near me. I believed I was strong, but strong is not always enough. Sometimes you just need a hug and someone to tell you it will be alright.

I had to wait a little while for the nurse to return. In the process I switched off my phone, lying on the bed reflecting about the mistakes I had made. Now it was time to move away and start a fresh life, something I'd always wanted to do. It had been a life-long dream waiting to come true.

When the nurse returned to me she checked my details and sat down on the bed. "Katrina," she said, looking at me and holding my hand. "I have this pill and this pill is the first stage of the termination. Once you take this there is no turning back." I nodded. "Then this pill you insert into your vagina and within ten minutes you will start cramping and the termination will start to happen."

"Okay." I nodded again as she let go of my hand, leaving the pills placed in the palm of my hand. I realised this was no joke and once I did this, this was it, there would be no turning back.

I sat on the bed plucking up the courage to take the pill. I took the pill out of the wrapper, looking at it in my hand. I took the pill.

I had two weeks rest from work and I thought about a lot of things, how I was living my life and how I wanted to live my life. My first day back to work I got up bright and early feeling refreshed and happy. I showered, got dressed, fed my cat Sherbert, made my way to the bus stop and got on the 183 towards Harrow. When the bus stopped at Kingsbury I took my chip out of my phone, opened the bus window and threw the chip outside. I took a deep breath and that was the end of me and Ricki. I have never seen him since. He asked for me but I feel leave the past in the past and what happened between us happened but leave it there. I heard he has a son now and I'm very happy for him and I hope he is happy too.

Me and Sunni; I can't tell you what it is but I keep a special place in my heart for him. I know he doesn't for me but everyone is different. I really hope one day I get to see him and we can have a good chat about the old days and the fun we had. He is someone I wished I kept a friendship with, he was a decent guy and whoever got to marry or date him is a very lucky girl.

Our lives have moved on now. I have changed and matured. I feel different and see life differently. If only back then I'd had the mindset I do now things would be so different, my life would have been so different. I was cold towards Sunni. It had nothing to do with him, it was just how I felt at that time. My heart cared less.

I still feel we had so much more to give our relationship if only I gave him a chance, if only he gave me a chance. Our chapter is over but what could have been is unwritten.

CHAPTER 11
WHY DO YOU HATE ME SO MUCH?

The smiles, oh the smiles can mask anything. Call me a whore, I'll smile. Call me a bitch, I'll smile. But call me beautiful and I really don't know how to smile!

This is where the abuse really started with my mum, well the time I remember the most. She was abusive when I was young but I was hardly home, roaming the streets, so I didn't care as much. And when you're young and occupied you don't care as much when your mum is calling you a bitch, you're too busy playing with your friends, calling them bitches cause that's all you know.

When my mother was drunk or high on drugs I would just leave the home and go to a friend's house or roam the streets all night. I know, not a nice thing for a young girl to be doing at the age of fourteen but that's all I was ever taught: "Get out of my face, get out of my house". I never felt I had a place called home.

It was when I got of age and started to see life differently. I was maturing. I got myself a job and wanted a career to better my life. This is when the madness began: the jealousy, the name-calling, the mocking, and the throwing me out on the streets. I was not worthy and I felt unworthy. Who could I turn to? Who could save me? I really felt abandoned.

This was the time in my life where I wanted to end it all.

Mothers, who would have 'em? Certainly not me if I could prevent it. I don't know what a good mother is supposed to be. Can someone explain to me please? I saw good mothers but I was not given one. No father and no mother you might as well say. I was given the short straw in life when God picked my parents. Even though they were there in body and flesh they were never there for me.

My mother was continuing to throw me out on the streets on a constant daily routine. It became the norm but not normal for me. I just wanted to sleep most of the time or watch television, you know, chill out in your home. Once, I would have been fifteen, my mum had been drinking throughout the day. Night-time came and everyone had gone home. I knew that I was going to get the brunt of her abuse and I was ready for it. God knows what she was saying, slurring her words, muttering, but I know it wasn't nice words like 'I love you Katrina'. I can't remember much but the next thing I know I was calling the police to take me away. I begged them, "Please, please, please take me away."

My mother told them to take me to my auntie's home, being all polite and non abusive. "What's the matter Katrina?" they asked me.

"I want to leave here, can you take me somewhere else please? Can you take me now?"

"Why what's wrong?"

My mother tried to butt in, to speak for me to divert the attention away from the subject of why I wanted to leave.

"I don't like it here and I want to leave for good."

Looking confused as to what had happened the police officers saw my mother was very intoxicated and thought there was a problem but didn't want to ask me while my mother was present. "Okay Katrina, we will take you to your auntie's house and in the morning we will come and see if you're okay. Is that okay? Are you happy going to your auntie's home?"

"Yes," I replied, not happy but I would get a good night's sleep and deal with what I needed to in the morning. I knew if I stayed at my aunt's home my mother could still get to me and I just wanted to get away from her as soon as possible.

It was a warm summer's day in 2003. I woke up really early, the sun ablaze, piercing through my bedroom window. We had great summers back in the early 90s when the whole community would be out for hours and the evenings were so sweet: the kids playing, the laughter, the drama, the parties on the back of the hill till the late hours. I could walk for hours, thinking, taking in all the feelings around me. I knew when I was older I would understand the value of these walks.

As I rose from my bed the house was ever so quiet. Sherbert my cat came running to me, meowing for food. "Morning Sherbs, you hungry?" She looked at me. Meow, which was a yes, purring and rubbing the side of her on my ankle.

I made my way downstairs. The house was always dusty with clutter everywhere and dishes around. I felt like I was living in a hole in the world and I just couldn't get out of this hole. I fed Sherbert her tuna. She was so healthy. She was called Sherbert Newman, a proper family member. She would only drink water and eat yogurts and her tuna, maybe a little snack now and again, but she got star treatment and I loved treating her. She was my saviour who made me feel happy. When my mum would shout down the house, she would run for cover or run into my room. Sherbert was bought for me by my mum. I was very grateful for Sherbert.

The day was so airy and beautiful, but it felt so strange. No appearance from my mum. God knows where she was but to be honest I didn't really care as long as I knew when she was returning. I knew by the time 8pm came I would be in serious shit and not because I put myself in it. My mum would be drinking and smoking throughout the day and I would face the brunt of it when she returned home. Most of the day I stayed home. I always loved staying in but was forced onto the streets. It's amazing how so much peace can come from someone not being in your presence. Relaxing about for most of the day, I then decided to head out as usual. I would link up with Lisa. I spent most of my time with Lisa, occasionally with my brother and other friends. I had different relationships with different people and I would act different with certain people. This was the acting in me, I would act like the crowd I was with. Bizarre I know but that's how I moved around life. I never liked it but I guess I didn't know how to act around people.

That evening I met up with Lisa. We started off drinking at her house then the Hendon pub, then Corks Wine Bar and ended up clear in South London somewhere with some guys we didn't know. I swear God had me covered on many occasions; the guys we would roll with would never do anything sexual to us unless we wanted to and they actually liked our company. We were very outgoing and very outspoken. Most of the time I was happy to be outside. At least if I ended up at someone's house I would get some sleep and that's how I thought, where can I lay my head? As long as I go out drinking and socialising I can get drunk and lay my head somewhere. I would be dreading going back home after hours. I knew what was waiting for me behind that closed door. I would try my best to stay out, but this night no one was really ongoing hardcore after Corks Wine Bar. That night I drank so much but drinking had became the norm of life so I wouldn't even get drunk. It would take me at least three bottles of vodka and a bottle of Jackie AKA Jack Daniels to feel the niceness. Any drink passed to me I was drinking, just to get as drunk as possible. It was time to leave. I felt nice enough, still able to communicate, and we headed home, taking the night bus to Leicester Square. It felt like the quickest but longest ride ever. I wanted the bus ride to end but also I didn't want it to end. Reaching my home stop West Hendon Broadway, I looked around thinking where can I go? There was nowhere apart from home. Fuck this I'm going. I will just go into my room and sleep; she can't bother me if I fall asleep.

The house was quiet, but the lights were on. I wondered if she was home. Opening the door in front of me was that face, sitting in the chair. The house stank of weed and a bottle of vodka was by her side. She was watching TV. Maybe she was cool and didn't want any trouble today, let's hope. I didn't say a word and entered my room. I sat on my bed feeling nice from the drinks I had prior. There was no sound, no movement. I headed to bed. It was 1am.

"Get up!" I heard a loud shout. The light came on. I was stunned and dazed being woken from my sleep. "You never cleaned your room, you never washed the dishes. Get up! Look at you, you slut, you whore, you bitch. You're sick in the head." Her eyes were bulging, glazed from the alcohol and smoking. Not again, I was thinking, jumping out from the madness I had just faced. She was screaming in my face, foaming at the mouth. I looked at the time not saying a word. 3am. This woman waited for me to get into a deep sleep so she could shock me out of it. Who does that kind of stuff? I looked at my mother in disgust and outrage. This is not normal but I had been facing this for such a long time it became natural. I don't remember when it started but I know it was soon after the passing of my grandparents. She marched out of my room, still mumbling at the top of her voice as if no one around could hear her, "Look at you, you think you're something special, you aborted two kids. You're a slut, this is my house and you abide by my rules."

Maybe I am a slut but monkey see what monkey do, I really wanted to shout out, but I would always freeze and not say a word. Once or twice I would answer back, but nothing too damaging, just to let her know. "You're playing mind games." She would tell me to leave the dishes, but when I came home scream at me for leaving the dishes, what a mind fuck. I don't know how I survived.

Unable to go back to sleep I would sit up till daybreak. I was on alert so she couldn't startle me like that again, but the next morning I would be so tired. This is why I couldn't keep a steady job. Not because of my work but the mental abuse I was facing at home. This became a reoccurring routine.

She drank and smoked, I was out of the house raving, living a completely separate life. I would fantasize about leaving and never returning. I had good days when she wasn't abusive, but when she did there was no one around to witness it, she got away with murder, literally blaming her behaviour on me, and people believed her. Forgive them, I asked the Lord, for they know not what they do.

The mental abuse was so overpowering I really didn't know whether I was coming or going. I would go out, come home early, go to bed and early morning by 3am my bedroom door would burst open. "You slut, you whore. Why do you never wash the dishes? Look at you, no one likes you, you show off." The humiliation, the insults. At one point in the madness I was going through friendships and relationships. It all had a knock-on effect and each and every time I was blamed for the abuse and insults. "It's you, look at you, you tramp, you bitch." I really felt those words every time they were said to me and I really missed my grandmother. I knew if she was still alive I would not be going through this, no way, not in a million years. My grandmother was my protector and she would not let anything hurt me. I missed her so much.

The abuse became a regular occurrence until one day I'd had enough of the abuse, enough of the name calling, enough of everything.

Helen's laughter was mellow in the background. I headed downstairs feeling hungry and thirsty. As I popped my head through the living room door I saw Helen sitting in her usual chair by the computer and my mum sitting on the sofa. If looks could kill I would have dropped dead on the floor. My mother was drunk and was fuming but wasn't saying a word. While I was sleeping Helen had spouted to my mum about how I had met Ricki through Syreeta. That was it for me, my mum had finally pushed me over the edge and that's what she wanted, her eighteen year-old daughter angry, finally speaking out. I blasted my mother. "You're worthless, I'm pregnant because you haven't been a mother to me." I had finally said how I really felt. "I want to get away from you, you're no good." I could finally breathe. She knew I was an adult now and was not going to take her shit anymore.

Moving around through life I was dating, partying, working, but not spending much time at my mother's home. She was still carrying on with her outrageous behaviour but couldn't deal with me how she would when I was younger. On this day I came home and this was it for me. After this incident I had to get out.

I was super tired and didn't want to stay out. I walked up the stairs towards my bedroom. At the top of the landing there she stood, my mother, swaying from side to side, eyes glazed. "Look at you, you think you're special. Look at you, you whore." She was so intoxicated. I was fed up of this and wanted to sleep. As I walked forward my mother barged me as I tried to walk to my room. That was it, I lost it. I grabbed my mother round the throat. "You bitch!" I screamed. "Die!" I dragged her into my bedroom, throwing her on my bed. "Die, die!" And then I blacked out. My mother told me my eyes went wide like I wasn't there for a second and I believe I wasn't, I was completely lost. I wanted my mother to go away, far away, away from this world. That's how I felt.

Squeezing her throat with full force I heard my name gently. "Katrina!" I let go of my mother's throat. Still very angry I started to smash up the house screaming, "I hate this house, I hate this world and I hate my mother." After my outburst I stormed out of the house.

I do remember in the midst of my outburst my mother on the phone. It could have been my auntie Shirley, because that's who she called when she would start on me and I retaliated in self defense. "She's just attacked me for no reason, I don't know I think she's on drugs." Crying down the phone to get sympathy. "She's tried to strangle me." God knows what Shirley said but I received a call from her as I was running away, trying to find my way out of this mess. The one thing I knew for sure was I never wanted to go back and I would find a man to get me out of the horrible situation I was in. He would look after me, he would keep me safe. That's what I thought but I was so wrong. I needed to be careful as I was so vulnerable and carefree. Anyone who showed me kindness I would attach myself to, not knowing the consequences.

I now know I must be careful who I let into my surroundings; not everyone is who they claim to be, not everyone is a friend. Get to know the person you make friends with and start a relationship with. It can cause catastrophic events if you let the wrong people into your life. It can cost you your well-being and your life, as I found out in 2007. Something I would come to regret later on in life.

I began to think about my life's choices and headed off to the council the next morning after roaming the streets all night. The council at that time was based in Hyde House in Hendon. Just my luck I knew the housing officer at the time. It was Mrs Baker's daughter, someone my mum grew up with and knew very well. She lived two doors away from the family home. I couldn't believe it when I saw who was behind the reception desk. "What you doing here Katrina?"

Shaking, tired and shy I just spouted out everything that was happening to me at home. Whether she believed me or not I couldn't hold it in any more. I was utterly exhausted. She was very shocked to see me there doing an application. I explained, "I can no longer live at home with my mother and need somewhere to live."

"Why, what's wrong?"

"She's abusing me and I can't take it anymore." Well that was a stupid thing to do. She grew up with my mum and who did she run to letting them know I had done an application for housing? Yep, so they dismissed my application, wheeling me in trying to sort things out with my mum. I refused but where else could I go? I was oblivious to the world, what I was entitled to, what help I could get. I didn't know what resources were available to help me.

So I ended up back at my mum's living in unpredictable times. When my uncle Keith moved to Manchester he asked me to go and live with him on many occasions but I said I was more attached to London. It was strange, I wanted to get away but not leave what I knew behind. That's the fear of life, it can scare you sometimes and make you not achieve your dreams or move on in life.

I started travelling to Manchester to see my uncle Keith. He was always my saviour, my way out. He kept me happy and always looked out for me. I would spend a few weekends in Manchester. I knew people up there as well so that was cool, somewhere I could chill out peacefully. I had great times in Manchester. My weekends would go so quickly when I was having fun.

Working long hours at Sunvally Amusements I did love my job, even though I was going through what I was going through at home. That's where I found peace and a little happiness. Going home was like hell on earth for me so I would ask for extra shifts just so I could be out of the house. My life started to feel a little bit nice but it was horrible going back home. I was raving most of the time and sleeping around at people's houses, washing the next morning and heading to work. When my mum didn't see me for a while, even though I was paying my rent, she would cuss me out, "This is not a hotel, go and stay where you were." It's like I couldn't win, but I still stayed in that terrible situation. I realised that's all I knew and didn't know any better, though I knew what was going on was wrong. Kind of baffling I know but that's how I felt. I was never taught anything and had to learn most of my things from the road or friends. I was literally like a baby in a grown woman's body. This gave people the advantage to take the piss out of me. I had knowledge and was intelligent, a gift God gave to me, but I never knew how to use it, so I mastered my gift by working out how the world worked and how people worked. Then I mastered me and that's how I got about for a few years and that got me by.

By the time I was nineteen my mother became notorious and more violent, challenging me to fights, puffing out her chest to me. Her favourite line on many occasions was, "You think you're something special, you think you're so nice. Look at you, you're dumb, you're stupid." So many times out of rage I wanted to kill my mum and it was building up. If she died at that point in life I wouldn't have even given a shit. The world would have been a better place without her evilness. Sometimes I would think why hasn't she dropped dead yet? I just wanted her out of my life.

I was starting to get fed up working to pay rent and coming home to abuse after twelve hour shifts when all I wanted to do was relax. I couldn't go every day to people's homes; sometimes I would just go home and deal with what I had to deal with. It was not nice but at least if I got an hour's sleep it was something.

I got my first tattoo when I was sixteen. Tattoos were as not common back then as they are now and I've had a few more tattoos over the years. Some sentimental, some just out of pure foolishness. I guess that was the decade when I was going through my life crisis. The pain from the needle somehow took the pain away from my home life problems. Once I had my first one, I couldn't stop. I have eleven tattoos all together placed all over my body.

Now I can't stand them and I'm getting rid of a few. Being a mother changed me and I feel I need to look more like a lady. I'm not saying women with tattoos don't look lady-like, but I feel like a lady and I've changed into a lady, and for me a big dragon tattoo doesn't make me feel lady-like.

I remember my first ever tattoo. Me and a girl I grew up with from the West Hendon estate both decided to go to Edgware Tattoo Parlour to get a tattoo. I wasn't really bothered getting one, I just followed suit but she was adamant she was going to get one. We were underage. The age for consent was eighteen and we looked like little school children. I don't know how we got away with it. Back then in the 90s no one cared really, you just did what you did. We made our way up to Edgware to get our first tattoos, getting on the number 32 bus excited about marking our skin. There was no turning back; we had hyped ourselves up so much on the bus. I think the adrenaline rush was exciting us even more. "What you getting?"

"I'm getting this, what you getting?" We were going through so many things and designs. We made up our minds, she was getting her name and I was getting 'Lil Kim' in a nice fancy design. They do say if you don't have good role models around you end up destroying your life; this didn't destroy my life but my skin.

Getting to the tattoo parlour there were a few people waiting as we looked at some images. "Can I help you?"

"Yes," we said. "I want a tattoo saying 'Lil Kim' and my friend wants her name."

"Okay, can you sign this consent form and we're good to go." The man never asked for our age or anything. The friend I was with was even smaller than me, you could clearly see she looked young; she didn't even look over thirteen to be honest.

"Let me go first," my friend stated.

"Okay." She was more on it than me and this was her idea so she went first. She was nearly shaking the table she was resting her arm on for the tattoo. It looked like it really hurt, but she held it down like a soldier and got through it.

I was next. Looking at her one it looked very long and bold but I was getting small writing at the top of my arm where I could cover it so I was cool. I was obsessed with Lil Kim so it was a tattoo for my G. I braced my arm down.

"You ready?"

"Yes." He cleaned up his area and opened a new needle. I didn't want to look so I turned my face away.

"Ready?"

"Yes."

"You sure?"

"Yes."

I could hear the needle getting closer and closer and closer with the buzzing sound. As he touched my arm I jumped. "No, no, don't do that."

"Okay, okay. Are you sure you're ready?" "Yes, yes."

"Okay, let's go." I kept as still as possible. I could hear the buzzing of the needle again getting closer and closer and closer. "Okay I'm going to do it." I felt a little pinch.

"Ouch!" I screamed out, keeping as still as I could while my friend laughed her head off in the back.

"That's not so bad is it?" After a while the pain wasn't too much and I soldiered through it. It was over within minutes. "There you go not so bad after all," the tattoo guy said to me. All chuffed with myself I went to look at my new tattoo in the mirror. I looked at it confused. The name was different and the style was different. How could he get that wrong? He put 'lilkim' all together with no space and a bit wonky. I was livid and pissed but still hyped I'd had the tattoo.

Heading home all excited that we had our first new tattoos we were so happy but to be honest they looked fucking shit. I can't believe we even paid for that kind of treatment, but we had them and I don't think we realised we had them for life. I soon got rid of that 'lilkim' tattoo and at eighteen I got my official legal tattoo and that was a dragon on my left upper arm which I still have to this day.

I was growing up really quick. I think I experienced things in life no child should so I was more advanced than other kids. I wasn't alone in my experiences though, and that helps when other people have similar circumstances as you, but you're all fucked because of your upbringing so you can relate through drugs and alcohol but not have a civilised conversation about how you feel or if you need help. It would feel strange to talk this way to each other but we could rave together, fight together, get man together. I think we were all feeling a type of way or very low but didn't know it.

Nineteen, I was branded so many things by this age: a thief, a liar, you name it they called me it and I didn't give a shit because I knew I was none of those things, but I knew who was. I was the one who was most loyal out of all of them and I believe they knew this so they tried to target the loyal, genuine one so people got distracted and missed their true character. That was when I started to pull myself away from certain people and then their true selves would be revealed.

Going through what I was going through was not helping my situation at home, when you're out with so-called friends who are slagging you off, degrading your name behind your back but to your face kiss your ass. I'm not that way inclined and if I see you're this way then I'll distance myself from you, because you are no good, and you are no good for me.

My mother was still drinking, still being abusive, but I was much older and wasn't backing down. I was giving it as good as I got with the cocaine giving me that boost of confidence to stand up for myself. Nobody knew the extent of the abuse I faced. I guess I'm lucky, my life could have been worse; I feel I still got a second chance at life even though my life is not picture perfect.

The rawness of the abuse started to stand out. It was triggering and I couldn't stand it anymore. I was turning twenty and I knew I wanted out so I started looking for a place to live. I was working and could pay for a studio flat or a room. I was planning to leave I just needed to save £900 deposit and up-front rent. I had saved a fair bit and was getting ready to leave.

But one night she either knew I was going to leave or she had an instinct. I know that everything I told Lisa she told my mother, so perhaps she told her. Why, I don't know, but she did.

I came home that night early. I was so tired from partying, staying up all night, drinking and taking drugs. I needed sleep. It was around 12am and I could hear the music playing as I approached the house. Here we go again, but I just didn't care; I needed sleep.

THE LOVE OF A MOTHER

My mother was dating Peter at this time and when he wasn't around or he pissed her off I got the full force of her shit but not today, not on my watch I was not having it. I took my key out and opened the front door, the music sounding louder as I entered. I couldn't see my mum anywhere but knew she wasn't far.

I slowly walked up the stairs. I got to the top and there at the top of the staircase stood my mum. "You," she said, "look at you, you think you're so hard don't you? Don't you?" Her eyes were glassy and she was slurring. Little did I know she was taking cocaine herself and was bang on it, which kind of made sense for her outburst behaviour.

As she continued with her abuse I made my way to my room and I attempted to close my bedroom door. "This is not your house, don't close that fucking door." Walking towards me my mother was face-to-face with me, angry, aggressive and ready to fight.

I can't remember much about what happened next but I do remember it felt like I was waking up. My hands were around my mother's neck and I was squeezing her neck so tight. She was trying to call my name. As soon as I came round I let go of her neck.

In utter shock but still angry I froze as my mother started to cough and gasp for breath. "You tried to kill me, you tried to kill me!"

Still hearing my mother's voice I lost it and started to smash up my room and the whole house, expressing my feelings of anger. "Die! Just fucking die!" I screamed. The rage in me even scared me. I was so angry. She had made me so angry that I wanted to kill her and that felt horrible.

I don't really like talking about those moments but it's a part of my life and I'm sharing it with you. My mother pushed and pushed me over and over again to the brink of despair to the point I was so angry I could have killed her. It's something I try to keep away from my memories and move on with love in my heart.

Soon after this incident she threw me out. I returned but the same old shit was happening, it was like she didn't learn. She also went around saying I had attacked her. That was it for me now and I could not take any more. I moved out officially and she still called for me to return home.

The man my mother started seeing, Peter, is my brother Benji's father. There was no introduction; I just used to see him in the house. It already didn't feel like my home and when he came over I knew I was going to be thrown out on the streets, and then it would be me who was subjected to an ordeal of abuse when he would fuck her over. This was constant for me. Sometimes she was home sometimes she wasn't and when she was not I was the happiest girl alive, but I still didn't get a good night's sleep because she could return home any second and God would only know what mood she was in.

Soon after my brother Ben was born I was forced to leave her home and was glad. It never felt like my home. In my heart of hearts I was happier than her to leave. She never made me feel like a daughter and I never felt the love of a mother so I was glad to be gone.

My brother's dad Peter did my mother over and basically had my brother Ben for his own convenience. Why? Who knows, but it was not out of love, and there was yet another black boy fatherless. In this case it was even sadder because my brother has complex needs. This should have given my mother the motivation to correct her mistakes in life but she still did not. Everything was and is about her. Why did she have children if she was not willing to be a mother? If she looks up the definition of what a mother is I can bet you £100 she is not one.

I watch my brother struggle on a daily basis and yes I believe my mother is to blame, not for my brother's condition but for not managing and giving the correct care to him. The help was there and is there, she chooses not to take it, but in the same breath is disrespectful and expects people to bow down to her after she has been slagging and talking about her family while watching Eastenders, Emmerdale and Hollyoaks. She loves to gossip about people but hates when people gossip about her. Isn't karma a bitch? I think she has life all wrong.

I stayed with my mother and brother Ben until he was one and a half. I was there helping my mother and she slowed down a bit with her abuse. Ben was there and she did not have the ammo she had before. There was a little baby in the house and he made the house peaceful. But she would still drink and be abusive and constantly hint that I needed to leave her home. I believe she didn't really want me as a child but wanted to get out of her family home from the drama and the only way was to get a council flat, but when she realised her mother had passed over and she now had to be a mother herself for real she was not willing to do it.

She was nagging and niggling even when I was working my ass off paying her rent. Nothing I did was ever enough and when I got things wrong, well, let's just say I was finished. There would be no point even trying to explain myself; I knew what was coming. "You fool." I knew I had to get out.

I tried with my mother and I do believe in second chances. She got more than that because that's how my heart is. No one is perfect and I know we all make mistakes. Just like I would like to be forgiven, I believe people should have that chance to make things right but if you continue to take the piss then it's not a mistake it's a choice. Mistakes you learn from.

I bought some jewellery from New York 14 carat gold. You could never get that kind of jewellery in London, it was beautiful jewellery and I bought it as my gift from the country and for investment for the future. I was going to give it to my brother Ben. It cost me over £1000.

I was heading to Paris with two of my friends for the weekend and decided to leave my jewellery at home, all of it. Biggest mistake. My mother took my chain and pawned it, she took my bracelet and pawned it, and she took my ring which was my birthstone and pawned it. Still to this day I'm very, very angry. She takes people's things and not just mine, she has a reputation for this and she is well known for stealing, but no one confronts her. I did. I asked her where my jewellery was. She blamed my poor brother Ben who could barely walk and my jewellery was high on my shelf in a tin. She didn't know I'd tested Ben before I left and I knew he could not climb the shelf and could not open the tin. Plus I had confirmation from the people she told she sold it for rent. What a piss taker. Well that's between her and God but I will not trust my jewellery around her, nor money.

That was very hurtful. Maybe she was jealous I was trying to have a life travelling the world which is one of my dreams. I could never have anything nice and if I did she would throw it away or steal it. No wonder I drank and smoked constantly; I still had to pay rent in a home I was not welcome in.

That was it for me; I had to leave her home. I was done. I ended up homeless in the city of London. Homeless does not always mean living on the streets, homeless means not having a home. Staying with people is very hard to do when you're mentally struggling and they can't help you and you can just about help yourself. Sofa surfing. People would offer their homes to me but that was chaotic and was just as bad as living at home; different people same kind of shit, so I left their home and found myself living with a friend for a little while until I got my own place.

When I was homeless I became pregnant and was ready to start a family but it wasn't my time and I miscarried. I take that as it wasn't my time and God had another plan for me. I dated around for a bit on and off for two years then soon after I met Awab we were soon to be married.

I have never looked back after moving out of my mother's house. I could never live with my mother again, young or old, the mental scars and abuse are still there so if I went back to live with her I would have a mental flashback of how it used to be and I would want to escape and get out.

I can see the world is changing and it's the end of an era. I believe in change but wrong change is no good, when it makes you feel like you don't have a voice and have no say and you've been told to put up or shut up.

The people of this world are destroying the beauty of it. There is no love, it makes me very sad to see that there once was so much love and now there is none. I just pray Kayleigh finds her way in life and God blesses her with good health, good friends, good living, a good home and a good life.

The kids of today have no unity and it is so wrong, too many different cultures, too many different people not wanting to unite. They have made this world and country difficult to live in. My time has come to leave and I want out. The food has changed, the air has changed, the people have changed and the crime has changed. We're living in a sick world full of hate and I do not like it. I was born and raised in the 80s and 90s and I can say they were the best years I have ever seen. Morals, respect, love, community, care and attention. Growing up in my community was great and we all had one another's back.

My mother left an emotional impact on my overall feelings from her abuse, how I see life and how I feel about people. The unwanted feeling has made me want to help people who feel alone and have no-one to talk to, people that need a helping hand. The hardness of my mother's love has turned me into a person I never believed was inside of me, a loving and caring soul.

I would like to thank me for never quitting no matter what I face, I continue to strive rising higher each and every time. With my knowledge and the power within me I'm ready to change the world.

I believed drink and drugs were my solution, to feeling better all the times I felt like giving up, I realized giving up was not in my blood.

CHAPTER 12
BEAUTIFUL PAIN

When the world is seeing beauty she walks around seeing a mist, colourblind to the world until God hits her in the one place she never wanted to open: her heart. Then all is revealed, the beauty of the world. Now she can see, now she is happy, now she sees happiness. She makes broken look beautiful and pain look unique. Everything looks black and white. As she looks through the world she's colourblind, a passionate pain of beauty, a love you cannot see through the pain of people. This kind of pain forms art. If you notice, most musicians, artists or writers when they're telling a story it's a painful experience but they turn their pain into beauty. Sometimes we must endure pain to see the beauty in ourselves and the world.

I never for a split second thought I would feel love, that beauty of love. You don't know how to respond to it so you try and love the first person who shows you interest because now you're ready for love. You're bursting to be loved. You look at the trees differently and can see the love within all over the world, sprinkling little bits everywhere for people to feel and watch the world light up with colorful souls through the beauty of pain. Experience can make you see beauty in the most devilish of people.

CHAPTER 13
DO YOU BELIEVE IN MARRIAGE?

Do you believe in karma? Well I'm a true believer in what you dish out is what you shall receive. Look how many people disclose their life story and most of the time it's about sorrow, always about money, sex, drugs and the lifestyle that they have led and it's usually not a good one.

Love comes from my Father, he is not about hate and destroying His children so what other forces are around us? Killing, destruction, rape, hate, fear, unloving people: there is only one culprit for this behaviour and that comes from a non-loving force.

2009 is a year I can never forget. It's a constant reminder of when I became unwell, and when you're trying to get better in a world or a relationship that is showing you nothing but negativity, how can you forget such a thing? This was the year I should have really run for my life but the softness of my heart kept me in a relationship that gave me no justice, no love, no care. Because I didn't let go of what was holding me back, I lost out on so many years of my life suffering endlessly at the hands of a man. I have always stated that men are my downfall. For some strange reason they treat me like shit.

Who in their right mind wants to get married? I know its God's plan and a part of his love. Uniting and producing life is God's philosophy.

I never thought in a million years I would walk down the aisle and say I do, but I always wanted to get married and have the perfect wedding in a beautiful castle or abroad on a lovely beach somewhere with all my family and friends present. A fantasy I would have liked to become a reality. I hoped on my wedding day when my husband looked at me he would see me as the most beautiful woman in the world. If he was able to stay calm then he wasn't the one for me, if he cried and held my hand

and we cried together then I would know he was my perfect soul mate, my main man for life.

I met Awab in 2005, two weeks after I broke up with Carlton Ebanks, an on and off relationship I'd had for two years. It was with Carlton that I fell pregnant and was unaware of it until I miscarried in his bathroom. Yet again something I had to keep to myself and deal with alone. It was something I was used to: hospital alone, appointments alone, you know the pattern.

I met Awab on a night out in a club called Pier One in Dalston. The club is no longer based in Dalston and looks completely different today, more modern and up and coming for the posh totty people moving in and pushing the urban scene out. You still have your scallywag people that come out as soon as it gets dark. They are like bats, only coming out at night. I do wonder where those people go in the daytime.

I was more relaxed at this time in my life and I knew what I wanted. I just didn't know how to get it. I was always thinking how am I going to get it and how am I going to move on? I had a few opportunities that came my way but I just didn't have the confidence to go forth with it and start again. It's like I needed a man to secure me. I know this because I liked being around men, men were my protection and I was always taught and shown by my uncles a man should be the king of his castle and take care of his family and woman.

So when I date a man I have high expectations. I never had a father present so if I decided to have children with a man I would expect him to be a man and work hard and be family orientated. If you can't meet those needs eventually I will take myself away.

I will not settle for anything less than what I deserve. I'm not saying I won't give a person a chance but it looks like when you do people take advantage of your kindness, taking it for weakness. They do not understand you are genuinely kind, and when you finally are fed up of their rubbish they start to cry, when you want to live your life how you choose and not for them

You can say that life can be one big mess. I'm so glad I'm clued up. God has always kept me that way. It's now I'm using the gift he has given

THE LOVE OF A MOTHER

to me and now I'm using it wisely and in a good manner and not to please or fit in with everyone else.

The night was so warm and I was wearing a white tracksuit. I had finally decided to finish it with Carlton so me and Lisa went to Pier One. I wasn't in the mood to party but that was the only option at that time; rave or stay in my mother's home. Yep, raving was much better. Me and Lisa were regulars at Pier One and became friendly with the owner. I was in a sour mood but still content and all I wanted to do was chill out. Standing by the exit doors were a few guys dancing near us. Unfazed, I was looking at one of them. I couldn't see the guy's face as it was so dark, but he came over to me asking for a dance. We ended up talking and dancing throughout the night, Lisa with one guy me with another, not knowing that three years later I would marry this man.

Talking and dancing, the night started to come to an end. Before I knew it, it was 5am, the club was playing its last song and Awab gave me his number. I gave him my house number. I wasn't even bothered if he called. I was so pissed off by then that I was not living a happy life or the life I wanted. If he called and she kicked off I would tell her to fuck off. And off we headed home.

A few days later, Lisa rang me. "Oiii, that fella."

"Who?" I replied. "What fella?" I had already forgotten about Awab as I was rolling around with a guy called Charlie, and I was having a good time. He treated me like a princess and he wasn't kosher but we understood each other. Charlie asked me to be his girlfriend. I said no. He would do anything for me. He gave me a key to his house; he picked me up from work in the Lexus convertible; he gave me his credit cards but I would never use them unless I asked him; he would take me to the finest restaurants, places I had never seen or been before, the best clubs. Everywhere we went people would look at us. We would go to events where footballers were and I never felt out of place sipping champagne with his friend Michael Essen. Girls were envious of me and I didn't even know why, I was just friends with Charlie.

Charlie had a soft spot for me but I just didn't have one for him. One night we were out and he had bought every single rose in the club, over

100 roses. The looks the girls gave me. I was so shocked. I asked him, "How the hell am I going to carry this?"

He said, "I will," and he carried the roses for me. He made me feel like a princess, a lady at best and it was fucking amazing, something I have never had or felt again. Charlie would open the car door for me, hold my hand, and take my jacket. I never spent a penny when I went out and I was always given money to go shopping the next day. Oh those days were so sweet.

Charlie gave me an offer to have his child and he would get me a home and look after me, even if we were not together.

Thinking of it now I would have been better off with Charlie or Carlton, who both offered me the same chance and I turned both of them down. For what? To marry a man who lies and doesn't even appreciate the things you do for him. We basically got married for all the wrong reasons and I think to myself I turned down the best opportunities: security, a home, a chance to at least be happy with someone who had my best interests at heart, and I blew it for someone I didn't understand, for someone who didn't give two shits about me. I think how my life could have been. I had many chances and I let them go. I used to be angry with myself but now I just see it as a learning curve, life's lesson, something you learn from.

Soon after, Lisa had rung Lordon, Awab's friend. She rang me telling me Awab was going to call my house phone. Lisa told him not to and left it at that, but she asked me if I could ring Awab to see if they would take us out tonight. I wasn't doing anything so I did, but Awab couldn't understand me and I couldn't understand him. That was good because we didn't meet up that night. I was wishing we wouldn't meet up at all; I still was spending most of my time with Charlie and having a great time.

One night Charlie and I decided to meet up at Pier One. We spoke on the phone and were in good spirits. I entered the club and to the left of me was Awab, standing there. He was hoping I was going to turn up and yes I did, but not for him. I said hi and sat down. He was asking me all kinds of questions but I wasn't in the mood to talk to him, I was waiting for Charlie, that's who I was rolling with, that's who I couldn't wait to meet. Awab asked for a dance and I refused, turning away, sitting down, wishing Charlie would hurry up.

Around twenty minutes after I arrived Charlie walked through the door. He spotted me and took my hand, walking to the other side of the room in the club. Drinking my glass of champagne I looked over for Lisa thinking she was behind me but she was nowhere to be seen. Shrugging my shoulders I carried on talking with Charlie.

As the champagne kicked in the music started to sweet us and we began to dance. Charlie gave me a sweet wine. We had never danced like that before. Closing my eyes I embraced the wine. I felt everything including this rocket about to launch. Yes, Charlie had a hard-on and I was enjoying the moment. Dancing so close, in a trance, I felt someone tap me on my shoulder, disturbing my dance. I looked up and saw a black figure with dreadlocks looking at me. Awab. What did he want? I didn't even know this guy and he came over to me like some fucking madman intruding my space and fucking up my dance. He tapped me and walked off.

Charlie was baffled and vexed because he was like, "What the fuck was that all about?"

I never lie about anything and I had never lied to Charlie but this madman came and tapped me on the arm and Charlie was so upset with me. He thought I had been with this guy and he'd caught me in the club. The more I explained the more he was angry and didn't believe me. That was it, my night was finished. Awab had messed up my night with Charlie.

I marched over to Awab. "What do you think you're doing?" He ignored me. "You're mad."

Lisa looked at me. "You're out of order." "Why? I didn't come here to meet him, I came to meet Charlie." Absolutely fuming I told Lisa to take me home. Charlie was upset and left the club.

Driving home I was ringing Charlie but he wasn't answering. I had just blown any chance with this guy and it was all for someone I didn't even know.

My relationship with Charlie started to fade away a bit due to that incident in the club. He didn't trust me afterwards. Maybe he had trust issues but it didn't help when Awab tapped me on the shoulder while I was dancing with him.

Soon after Charlie got a girlfriend and I was cool with that. There was no bitterness and we had started to communicate again. He would still come and see me but we stopped going out together. I respected he had a girlfriend. He was a bit shocked I didn't fight for him, but I believe you shouldn't fight for love, love is natural and if you choose to move on then so be it, anyone that wants you to fight for their love is insecure. If I tell you I love you I mean it, if I want to spend time with you I mean it; it will be up to you how you respond to it.

It was Christmas day and I was on a go slow, fed up of life and men, working my ass off so I could relax for Christmas. I was chilling at my auntie Shirley's with the rest of the family. While everyone slept from the heavy Christmas dinner I was wide awake, looking through my phone. I came across the name Awab. His number had been in my phone for months and I had not acknowledged it. You see what boredom can do? I wish I'd picked up a book or called someone else. Why I called him I don't know. But I did. I called him.

The phone started to ring and Awab picked up. "Hello," I said.

"Hello who's this?"

"It's Katrina. I bet you don't remember me."

"Yes I do. Merry Christmas. What you up to?" Awab was heading home, he spoke to me as he went to go and meet his family. We had a nice conversation, short and simple. Now he had my number and my attention; I had let him into my life.

I had told Awab my birthday was coming up on 29th December. He said he was going to take me out and I said yes, but when my birthday came I changed my mind and I went out with my friends instead, eating lobster and drinking champagne, as you do.

Awab was upset with me as he stated on the phone later on. He said he was going to take me shopping and take me out. I never thought in a million years he would hold that against me when we starting dating, but the truth always reveals itself later on in life or later in the relationship.

I was still living at home at this point, but my mum was slowing down with her abuse and I wasn't home much, I was working and keeping myself occupied, and she had Peter who kept her occupied. I was twenty-two now and I had a voice - she couldn't deal with me as she would when I was younger and she wouldn't show her true colours to the man she was dating, so it was easier for me when she was with him. She would stay out for hours and I would be able to get peace and quiet and some sleep.

Awab would call me often and we would talk on the phone frequently, but I wasn't really interested in meeting up. I loved talking on the phone, I just love a good old natter. Even to this day if I have something to say I've got to talk it out. My auntie has a name for me, she calls me Talk Talk because when I get talking on a sweet subject you are not stopping me till you say 'bye I'm going to bed'. This is who I am. I love a debate and interesting talks. I like to know what people think.

Finally after so much talking and putting off meeting up I decided to meet Awab. He told me to dress nice, he was taking me out for dinner. Getting dressed it was such a warm evening and I was pre-drinking, listening to music. I was in good spirits and was in a happy mood. I got dressed for my date and my taxi arrived. I headed out to meet Awab. Back then a taxi cab from West Hendon to Ladbroke Grove was £8. You could never get that in this day and age, might be about £25 now, a bloody joke.

It was such a beautiful evening. I was thinking maybe he is the guy that's going to change everything, but I wasn't feeling him. However, I was willing to give him a chance. To this day I really don't know why him and not the others. I believe people deserve a second chance but I have come to understand that there should be no chances in love; unless it feels right don't do it. This is what I have learned the hard way.

People hold grudges and will try to destroy your life and well-being to fit them so you lose everything. Love is a powerful feeling, love is special. I have now found out love is meaningful. It can be so beautiful, love can be so sour but love can make you see the light and love yourself. The heart has more meaning, it's more than just keeping us alive, and the heart is the centre of everything, it's more than just life.

I arrived at Ladbroke Grove at the flat he was renting, well, he told me it was his flat and he was renting it: the first lie. If you lie to me from the beginning I will never trust you. A lie will continue and a person will feel it's okay to lie to you if you entertain it and allow it from the start. This is why I'm in the situation I'm in today, I allowed too much nonsense, thinking it was caring or they didn't want to hurt my feelings. No, a lie is a lie.

Awab was staying on Blag Grove Road in Ladbroke right by the Portobello Market. His flat was situated at the top and had the best view and the best breeze in the summer nights.

As I arrived I called Awab to let him know I was downstairs. I heard above me a window opening. "Look up," Awab said. I rolled down the cab window and looked up. There he was smiling, his big head out the window with his locks dangling down. This was another thing, I thought rasta was humble and genuine but this pussyclart wasn't, he was hiding the true him behind his locks. "I coming!" he shouted in his Dominican accent. Rushing down the stairs he opened the front door. "How much?" he asked the cabbie. He paid and I got out.

"Hi."

He was just smiling and I was smiling too. The evening was so warm and nice and I was happy to be out of the area and around something different.

"This is my flat," he told me, but he didn't tell me how he got the flat. You see in life people can give you the wrong advice. It's best you just stick with yourself and be real. People can mess up your shit. Awab's friends told him to tell me it was his flat but it wasn't, it belonged to a woman whose mother brought him up in England. He told me this was his family. Even when we were married he still maintained this was his family, but little did he know people talk and I found out that they weren't. I found out a few things and why I stayed with him I don't know, but I do know he is one lucky fucker. I don't give people chances like that. Maybe he's like my brother's mum and liked to put potions on people to keep them. Who knows? But I do know he is not my type and I stayed with him longer than I should have. He was just a fuck to me; I don't know why I married him and why I stayed with him so long. It baffles the fuck out of me every day and it baffled the fuck out of everyone I know. Maybe the love potion was poured into my food.

Awab escorted me up the stairs, two flights to his flat. The flat was nice but the entrance to his flat was a bit run down.

There were three other flats in the building. I checked out his home, it was a studio flat, open plan, not bad I thought, big enough for him.

While I stood in the living room/kitchen/ hallway, Awab grabbed his wallet and keys. "You ready?"

"Yes," with a big smile on my face. This guy actually made an effort and didn't look too bad, but he wasn't my type of man so I wasn't going to be in this for the long run.

As we headed out of his flat, I stood outside the building waiting for a cab, but no we were only going round the corner. So the restaurant is in his area I thought to myself, frowning. Okay, I haven't got far to walk, which was nice as I didn't feel like walking far.

Walking a short distance literally round the corner from his flat there was a Thai restaurant, very nice and in a secluded area. The street was so vibrant and filled with people on their journeys and I felt the good vibes being down in West London.

The restaurant was a fancy Thai restaurant. I hadn't been to a Thai restaurant before so this was a nice experience for me. Back then I was so skinny I was size eight with small boobs and a cheeky smile, I kept my hair slicked back and wore a gangsta coat. I really thought I was well hard.

By now I had stopped taking cocaine and slowed down on the alcohol. I was more relaxed but could see the effects the cocaine had on me. I was very energetic even though I'd stopped taking it. But I was thinking straight and was more focused and very calm and I was ready to start dating properly in a serious relationship. I wasn't attracted to

Awab and he's not the typical guy I would go for but he seemed nice so I gave him a chance. He was being very charming and sweet and I fell for that sweetness. I wasn't looking for a long-term relationship with him but I was just getting back out there on the dating scene to see how it was and to get myself ready for when the man I really liked crossed my path, then I would be ready to love him.

That night was very romantic and nice. I felt like a lady, something I have felt a few times but I never gave those other guys a chance. This time had to be true, this time I would give it a go even if he wasn't my type. We would see where this would take us.

We continued to see each other regularly then he asked me to stay the week. I jumped at the chance. Why not? He had a nice one bedroom flat high up in Ladbroke Grove. What more could I ask for? He was working most of the time and I would have the house to myself. When I was at work he was at work and when I was at his house he was at work and would return late that evening, so I slept and it felt like heaven getting to watch TV, lying in bed or lying on the sofa. It was sweet.

That week flew by and it was time for me to return home. "Why don't you come and live with me? Awab stated while I packed my bags to leave and go home. I had my own place in Camden town and felt comfortable enough to stay with awab long term I didn't have any friends over to my home and I became more distant from my friends when I spent more of my time with awab when we began to dating.

A few days later after work Awab picked me up with my stuff and dropped my stuff at his home. I had only a few things because I wasn't too sure and if this didn't work I could always go home. We were getting on ok-ish and he wasn't being a horrible person he was being very nice and caring.

Months passed and I had been staying with Awab enjoying our time together. I would wake up in the morning to love poems and teddy bears next to me in bed. He would surprise me with a few things but mostly love letters saying how much he loved me. Very sweet but my cousin would say cheesy. I felt they were very sweet and what he was doing was very sweet. Those were the days. So I gave up my flat and moved in with Awab.

We had such a laugh. His friends came and I invited a few friends and my family over. We partied and were having a good time together, still getting to know one another. Awab had a little daughter. She was living in Dominican Commonwealth West Indies, the birth country of her father. It never crossed my mind that he'd upped and left his daughter because I met him here, but he left her at such a young age, the age of three and never looked back. He would talk to her on the phone but never went back to visit her. That really wasn't my problem but I do feel bad for her, that can't have been nice for her. She's eighteen now and she wishes to have a relationship with her father but he's not really interested. You can see he has been here long enough to do more or even send for her but he doesn't. I look at Kayleigh and think I wonder if he would do the same to our child?

We were having a blast and I was more focused than ever. I thought yes maybe this can work and this is the man for me. I had been living with Awab for a year. I changed my job and was working for Aquifer Nursery in West Hampstead which was ideal, one bus ride to and from work. Sometimes Awab would drop me at work and collect me but most of the time I would take the 328 bus from Westbourne Park station in West London.

I was comfortable and life was starting to feel okay. I was a little bit happy. We had our little quarrels, ups and downs which couples do, but we got on and we enjoyed each other's company, when people weren't trying to get involved in our relationship.

I had been working at Aquifer Nursery for eight months. My wage was nice and I didn't have many bills to pay. £1,200 after tax wasn't bad and I was just working Monday – Friday 8am till 5pm. The weekends were mine and I had money to flex on. Awab had a decent wage as well so we were doing okay and living nicely.

Christmas came and I spent Christmas with Awab and his friends. Even that was nice, something different. I thought Awab was going to take me out somewhere nice for my birthday, or even a decent rave. I ended up at his friend's house for a drink up. It was his friend's birthday so I spent my birthday at Awab's friend's house, celebrating his friend's birthday. I still went and sat there thinking what the fuck am I doing here drinking while Awab acted like a clown, getting drunk, rolling on the grass or the pavement or letting his trousers fall down his ankles. Pure clown shit. He was thirty-one years of age but was acting like he was sweet sixteen.

Maybe it was that foolishness that kept me there, for the jokes. But jokes and playing are for a time and a place not constant, and Awab was constantly laughing and playing games. He was not a serious character so if you wanted a future with Awab it was best that you thought again. He wanted kids but did not want to look after them. No foundation or a future, Awab just floats through life and whoever he meets he meets and that's it.

That was one year he caught me off guard but he wouldn't catch me off guard again. My birthday would be spent nicely in a proper place.

Christmas passed and it was a lovely time, now it was back to work. Awab had mentioned to me that his visa was soon to run out and he needed to renew it. I hadn't paid much attention to Awab and his status but he needed to renew it to stay in England. While I was enjoying our time together Awab and his people were plotting to get him to marry me. A few of Awab's friends had made comments which enlightened me. "Why don't you just get married?" Married? I thought, no way, I don't even know him enough to get married, they must be joking.

Starting our second year of our relationship I bought my first car, which I purchased off my neighbour, a little runaround to get me to and from work and run a few errands. I crashed it after working a twelve hour shift. I was overly tired. I'd picked up Awab and dropped him at his friend's house. Driving home, I skidded on black ice and crashed into the barrier. I couldn't believe it, but it woke me up quick. I was lucky. Where I crashed my work colleague was sitting in a car and helped me. I still drove my car home and had to get the bus to work in the morning.

I soon bought my second car, a BMW. After rinsing that car out I settled for a Peugeot and enjoyed that car very much. It was a nice ride, didn't take too much petrol and had cheap insurance. However, due to my balance disorder I had to get rid of my car as I was unable to drive. I really miss my car, it helped a lot getting around especially when you have a child.

Our lives were running smoothly. I was keeping away from nonsense drama and dramatic people with their dramatic lives. I still would go out but not often, I was more at home.

Awab applied for his visa. I'm not too sure when but he came to me looking very down.

"They refused my visa."

"How come?"

"Because I didn't attend my college course."

"Oh no, can't you appeal?"

"No it showed I never turned up to the course so I have to go home."

Shit, I thought. If he went home I'd lose the flat; I wasn't down on the tenancy. Awab had never mentioned that he didn't have status. This renewal was the first time I had heard of a visa and leaving the country. I didn't say a word, all I was thinking was I needed to get my act together fast. I was pissed off and very upset he had kept that from me. I should have asked more questions but I was thinking to myself if you have a council property you must be kosher in the country, which would be impossible.

I left that where it was and didn't even think about it again. If it came to it I had a good job and money, I would go and rent somewhere. I never asked him about his status in England again.

In February 2007 I never saw all of the drama coming my way, but I had faced my fair share of it already; when my family saw Awab my mum was fuming. "There's something about him," she would say. "I don't like him." I just ignored her, she was always bitching and moaning and I'd had my fair share of abuse from my mum. Whatever she said didn't mean shit to me but she didn't hide her feelings, broadcasting it to the world and its army, so everyone knew I was dating a Caribbean man and he was luring me into his trap. The first thing my mother thought was he was going to use me to get status. For once in her dysfunctional mind she was fucking right.

It was February 14th, 2007: Valentine's Day. I was working a late shift and after work decided to go to Sainsbury's in Kilburn Park to pick up my champagne. This was just for me, I wanted to treat myself. I didn't think Awab was going to do anything special so I was taking my time to get home. Conversing with Awab throughout, he was rushing me to get home. "I'll be there soon."

If I remember correctly this day was a Wednesday. Two more days and I was off work for the weekend. I arrived home at 8pm. There were flowers on the kitchen table and in the bedroom were red, scented candles and a bottle of pink champagne. "Hi," he said with a big smile on his face.

"Hi."

"I've run you a bath and bought you your champagne and some lovely flowers." I was frowning but didn't think anything of it because it was V-day, but he was acting a bit strangely.

I went and had my bath, chillaxing with my champagne which was so nice. After my bath I was feeling very merry from the bottle of champagne I had just drunk. I lay on the bed drying myself. Awab pulled out some massage oil and started to massage me. Now I was overly relaxed and in a lovely zone, almost asleep but semi-conscious, enjoying the massage.

Awab was muttering to me, I was responding with "umm mmm". The next thing he stopped and I woke up out of the zone I was in.

"Katrina can I talk to you for a second please?"

"Yes," I replied as Awab gulped his glass of red wine. "You know I love you."

"Mmm hmm."

"You know we live together."

"Mmm hmm."

"Well," he said, as he reached for his pocket and bent down on one knee, "will you marry me?" For the first time in my whole entire life I was speechless. For a split second it felt good. Someone had proposed. I was feeling so nice and didn't think twice about his immigration status. "Yes, yes I will marry you."

That night was wicked. We drank until we got drunk, cracked jokes until we couldn't laugh anymore and had sex so many times we out-sexed ourselves! Over six times. If I had sex like that now I would end up like the letter W or in A&E fully mashed up. When age creeps up on you so do the pains and aching joints.

So now we were engaged but I was keeping this to myself. I couldn't tell my family, they would have objected to it straight away.

We'd been living together already nearly two years into our relationship so why not? I went for it with open arms but never knew what I was getting myself into.

Awab had to return to Dominica to sort out his status from there while I stayed behind working and sending him money. Awab's friends knew about us getting married but no one else, I held that down for a few years.

Living by myself was nice. I slept the whole time he was away but this was where the drama began. His friends were bitching about him and trying to stop me from marrying him. Why? I thought. They were supposed to be Awab's friends. So I paid them no mind, but they would tell me he was an alcoholic and they found him on the roadside in Dominica and brought him here, something I would find out later was true. And the people he would call his family weren't his family, he lied to me. They were telling me all about him setting me wise but I found it ever so strange that they were telling me this now while he wasn't here. We had been living together for over two years laughing and joking and nothing was ever said to me. I just thought they were being bad minded so I kept doing what I was doing and kept that information to myself. I didn't know that they were also slating my name to Awab. He kept this from me but kept them around me, maybe to keep an eye on me.

After those deep conversations about Awab I kept my distance from his friends and started doing my own thing. Awab soon returned and we would have to set the wedding date soon for him to get his stay in England.

Awab came back to England in March and our wedding date was set for November 29th 2007 at Wembley Town Hall. I was working my ass off and sorting out our wedding stuff. Back home the pressure was on. Awab was no longer working and I had to sponsor him for two years so everything was on my head. I had never paid a bill in my life, this was where I was thrown in the deep end and I handled my shit. I got to grips with it fast. I was managing my finances and my personal life and was trying to sort out a marriage in secret. The stresses of life were coming upon me and I did bring this upon myself trying to help someone out. When I think about would Awab have done that for me? Most probably not. Actually to be frank there's no way he would do that shit for me. My heart was too soft and I would always feel sorry for people who would never give me the time of day. But that has all stopped now. I'm not heartless, I've just learned how to use my heart less, ya dig?

Our wedding was coming up and our solicitor had our passports and Awab's money. It was October and he was getting the run-around. We had moved out of Ladbroke Grove and were living in Northolt. We did have a home but were soon to be homeless and about to get married. One of the stupidest things I have ever done but I still stuck by Awab, I felt he needed my help.

We still didn't hear anything from our solicitors in regards to our passports and we needed them in a couple of weeks, so we decided to go to the solicitor's office. When we got there the office was full of people waiting. It was strange, it was so full. As we asked to speak with Avni our solicitor the receptionist huffed, "You're here for Avni as well?"

"Yes."

"Oh no, take a seat."

I looked at Awab, Awab looked at me. At first I thought something had happened to Avni but that was far from it. Avni had stolen all his clients' money and taken their passports. We were shocked but lucky for us the police had our passports. The money we weren't too worried about, we just needed our passports.

The date was set to be married and now the passport drama was out of the way it started to run as smooth as it could. We were still going ahead with the marriage. Awab was doing little jobs on the side and he bought me my wedding dress, which was a lovely dress, for under £100. Our wedding was a cheap one. It was a cold winter's day and I only invited two of my work colleagues and Awab invited a few of his friends and that was it. Considering it was a rubbish wedding we looked good.

However, there was a problem with Awab's information. They refused to marry us unless I had my bank statement to show proof of address, so I had to go to Wembley Nationwide Building Society in my wedding dress. Everyone was watching me like what the fuck you're getting married and you're in the bank? They looked at me strange but gave me compliments. I felt like a fool, that day was awful for me; I would never do that again. Being young and naive can make you do some outrageous things. I managed to get my bank statement and they consented to our marriage.

If they hadn't that would have been it for us: no marriage, no Awab in England. It was me who saved his ass a few times and the thanks I get for it is abuse, more abuse and I'm selfish? I don't know anyone in this world that would do that, no one in their right frame of mind.

The ceremony happened. "I now pronounce you man and wife." I didn't feel like a wife and never have. "Now you can kiss the bride." And that was it, we were married. We signed the paper and we were officially husband and wife. Not the fairy-tale wedding I was supposed to have. For the honeymoon we went home and watched Eastenders.

I woke up the next morning feeling no different; I was still Katrina Cassandra Newman. Heading off to work was normal. People could not believe I had just got married. They knew something was up and they knew that it was not a genuine wedding or a genuine marriage. So many people, even people I didn't know, were upset with me for doing what I did and now I get it, it was wrong and I didn't get married out of love. My marriage was not good and we had a rough ten years together. Yes we made it to ten years but it was horrible. The blessing from my marriage is my daughter and regardless of the situation I really tried to make it work but it did not. A marriage like that wouldn't work and God will never allow sin to prosper.

In January 2018 I was officially divorced from Awab. When I explained to him I was divorcing him he said to me, "You're not fucking up my life." So I'm guessing for real the marriage was a sham and only for his benefit. The final and last straw for me was once I filed for divorce. After all I had endured throughout the relationship and marriage, I took Awab out for dinner. I wanted us to be amicable and good parents to Kayleigh. I explained to him that I no longer had feelings for him and I wanted to be happy now. Awab replied with a straight face while twisting his locks, something he does when he feels nervous, "The reason why I never decided to have a future with you, buy a house together, save together, is because I didn't know my future in England." Out of everything he had said to me to be so hurtful, that just finished me off completely. I finally knew that he was just in a relationship and if it worked out it worked out and if it didn't it didn't. That was his attitude and it all made sense to me. I was wondering, why is he not trying to do better in this relationship, and all the time he had other plans and in the meantime I'd put my life on hold and suffered at his expense. That was beyond repair for me. No one and nothing can ever change my mind to be with this man again. I will be civil but that's as far as it goes. Ten years was more than enough for me to be in a marriage that was going nowhere and I refused to do another ten years. I got nothing from the marriage and I have to start living my life from scratch. I have to start all over again but I'm looking forward to it.

I was very upset with myself. It cost me my time, my life and my wellbeing, but I have learnt so much from this. I know if I'd had the correct foundation this would never have happened. I teach my daughter daily to love herself and she is great. I don't want her to feel unloved, it can have devastating consequences. You live, you love and you learn.

THE LOVE OF A MOTHER

Me and Awab on our first date 2006

KATRINA CASANDRA NEWMAN

Me and Awab on our wedding day,
Brent Town hall Wembley 29th November 2007

Marriage is a gift from God to us the Quality of our Marriage is
Our Gift back to Him. I believed marriage was for life.

CHAPTER 14
THE DAY I NEARLY DIED

You know the saying, 'you know your true friends when you hit rock bottom'. It's such a true statement, but most of all you know your true family.

My life was changing and I knew what I wanted out of life and where I wanted to be, but I was always being drawn back to the people who didn't have my best interests at heart. I went down the wrong path with the wrong people and I know for sure my lifestyle had a major part to play. I was floating around drinking, partying, you name it I was doing it. I put myself in situations I would never even dream of doing now and for sure my daughter will not be doing that.

You're about to die and your mother says to your husband, "There's nothing I can do, call an ambulance," while she sits and eats her Sunday dinner. You see, people think it's easy to forgive, well it's not easy. When someone is so heartless and bad-minded towards you how do you forgive? If it wasn't for courage and wisdom I would be a broken woman with no soul. I remember it like yesterday - how can you forget when you nearly meet your maker?

Before I had Kayleigh, I fell pregnant in 2009. One night Awab wanted to go out. "Why are you doing this?" I said lying on the sofa. "I don't want to go out."

"Why not?" Awab replied.

"I just don't, I'm pregnant and I'm not feeling too good."

"Come on, it will do you good." Awab was being persistent, knowing full well I had just come from the hospital where they had told us there was no heartbeat from the twin babies I was carrying. I just wanted to stay home and rest. I was staying in the family home, which now my uncle and cousin owned. That evening I was so distant, a bit dazed but still fully functioning. It had not sunk in that I was going to lose my unborn children. I didn't feel pregnant anymore and all the sickness had gone. My belly was not getting any bigger but I still had hope because this time, for the first time in my life, I was ready to be a mum. I was ready to serve my children, be a wife and have the happy ever after I was looking for.

Distracting myself I asked Awab what clothes he was wearing to the party, still adamant I was not attending. Running up the stairs Awab fetched his clothes for the party which was a family friend's party down Ladbroke Grove. Ironing Awab's shirt I was in my own world, praying it was not true. I handed Awab his shirt to him as he came out of the shower. "You still not coming?"

"No Awab, I told you I don't feel well." "Come on, your brother's driving, it will help you." Awab wanted to rave so much but if he left me home it would look so bad, but he cared more about himself and partying and not me and the unborn kids I was about to lose. He was so cold and only comforted me when he was talking about partying, never 'how are you feeling', never 'let me run you a bath', or 'get some rest, I'm here for you'. But growing up feeling unwanted it was normal so when it was shown to me I would expect it, like it was okay to be treated in such a way.

After a few cuddles and brainwashing I decided to head out. My heart was not in it and why I left I don't know, but I did. Awab was so excited about partying. I just watched him laugh and joke with my brother and his friends, and I didn't say a word.

Driving to the party my brother was driving like a maniac and going over humps so hard, it was bouncing me up and down with no consideration for my health. I had to beg my brother to slow down while Awab sat there saying nothing, most probably thinking he's your brother why don't you tell him? I knew from the time I entered my brother's car that something wasn't feeling right.

Getting to the party I said hi to a few people and Awab said hi to a few people. I chilled, just standing by the back in my own zone, not being my usual self, while Awab, my brother and his friends enjoyed the party. I couldn't wait for the party to end and when it did I just wanted to go home. when the party had ended people were still chatting away outside, I was so upset so I told my brother and Awab I was ready to leave the party, but they didn't want to leave and I was adamant so we left. I was in so much pain in my stomach, I think the mad driving my brother did brought it on, and now my sadness turned into anger. When I'm angry you better just leave me alone or run. I don't remember how it started but it was like I blacked out and the next thing I remembered was Awab strangling me in the back of my brother's car outside my auntie's home, me crying in full blown anger mode.

I remember saying to him, "You say you're bad and you come so fucking quick," but before I could say the next sentence his hands were around my throat, squeezing my neck. That's the real Awab, that's the Awab no one saw apart from me.

Dropping off a few people Awab and me were still arguing on the way home. My brother sat there not saying a word, he doesn't get involved in my domestics and that's okay, I don't expect him to. I fight my own battles.

Getting back to my uncle's home, we were still arguing and I was angry, feeling he was not supporting me, he was not there for me. Shouting through the house I headed upstairs and Awab followed. Standing by the bed face-to-face, I hit him. We began to fight, well, me hitting Awab and him trying to hold me off. He then pushed me down onto the bed and braced his foot upon my stomach. "Stop it! Stop it!" Awab shouted, but I was so gone by then all I wanted was to hurt him how he hurt me, and the only way was to shed his blood.

Managing to get up I grabbed a bottle off the dressing table and threw it. It just missed Awab's head so I started to throw all kinds of things as he ran out the room. I grabbed one heavy perfume and without thinking I threw it with all my force, and I'm a strong black girl, there's power in my punch. I let it go and it went flying past Awab's face, just skimming him and smashing through the wall, leaving a massive gaping hole. I froze. I knew I was beyond my level of anger and I would do this man some damage.

I stopped. No tears, no nothing, just cold and numb. I sat on the edge of my bed thinking what is going on with my mind? What is going on with me?

I never spoke of my feelings but I expect people to at least have a heart. If you want me to do all these things, be there for you, babysit, lend you money, change my life, then a little bit of support is all I ask for. I never ask anyone for a thing but when people need me I'm always there. Life's a bitch.

That night the house was airy and me and Awab didn't speak at all, so I headed off to bed thinking my relationship was over. I wanted to move away. I was going to go and start afresh in Manchester and this time I was definitely going, there was nothing left here for me and the one person I knew who genuinely loved me would help me get on my feet. He has always stated, "Don't worry Katrina, I'll look after you." My main man, my uncle Keith, he has never let me down.

The next morning you could smell the strong smell of the perfume I had smashed the night before. There was glass and water all around the house and the top landing where the perfume fell from the hole in the wall. Awab was sitting quietly downstairs; I guessed he had sat up all night. Maybe he was thinking what I was thinking, this was becoming too much for me and he might as well forget this relationship. But Awab never speaks about how he feels so I will never know his true feelings.

Looking at the hole in the wall I wondered, how am I going to explain this to my uncle? I couldn't say I tripped and fell, by the impact you could see that it was a throw. I cleaned up the mess and looked for wall plaster; my uncle always had paint and decorating stuff around the house. I found some and this is what got me and Awab talking - there was no way I could reach that and fix it, so I explained to Awab, "Mate listen we got to fix this otherwise we're both fucked." Barely opening up his mouth he started to mix the cement.

I went back into the bedroom to lie down. My belly started to really hurt and the pain was like a period cramp and that's when I knew, it was happening. I was miscarrying. I was told don't call the ambulance unless it was serious and miscarrying was normal. I was told to go home and the babies would come out naturally.

As Awab fixed the wall, sanding it down, painting it, bringing it back like nothing had happened, the pain started to become more and more painful.

My uncle returned home from going out all weekend. He knew something was up; it was like he could feel it in the air.

I was feeling so unwell. Awab came into the room. "I'm going by Michael's." Yet again leaving me in pain.

I said, "Okay," as I clutched my belly, rolling back and forth. I wanted some water so I headed downstairs. The pain was unbearable. Awab left the house but I knew this miscarriage was not easy. I had never felt this pain before. I called Awab back. "I'm in so much pain."

"But I'm going to Michaels" he shouted angrily and upset he was going to leave me weak and in pain, I think he noticed I was in a bad way so he ended up staying.

Lying in my bed in excruciating pain I held my belly tight. As I pulled the duvet off I looked down at my pants. I was covered in blood. It was all over the bed. Awab pulled my pants off and blood poured down my leg, just gushing onto the bed. I asked Awab to help me into the bathroom. The blood was pouring out of me, I thought I was dying. There was so much blood everywhere. I was frightened, scared, shocked, but still held my composure. After twenty minutes of the blood just pouring from me, I collapsed. Awab ran downstairs to call my mum. I asked Awab, "Where is my mother?"

He replied to me, "She said 'what can I do? Call the ambulance.' She's not coming."

Wow. What could I say to that? If God took me that night I wonder how she would have felt. Maybe she would be happy that she wouldn't have to see my face anymore. That's how I was feeling

I was haemorrhaging and could have died from the blood loss. There was blood everywhere: the bedroom, the bathroom, Awab and me were covered in blood, but God had a different plan for me and kept me going. He kept me alive and I love him for that. I value my life so much now, I really do.

Panicking, not knowing what to do, my uncle Stephen called for an ambulance. My uncle was so panicked he forgot my name, asking Awab, "What's her name again?"

It was so distressing for me but I can't imagine how they felt seeing me in such a state, thinking I was bleeding to death. I managed to stand up, holding on to Awab as I pushed out the two sacks. By then I had no more life in me and once I had pushed them out I collapsed to the floor. The bedroom door opened and the ambulance crew came through the door. The first thing they said was, "She's going to need a blood transfusion."

I was so exhausted I just wanted to rest, but I was so relieved that I wasn't feeling any more pain. That pain was something else, that pain was worse than birth pain but I got through it, by the grace of God.

Heading to the Royal Free Hospital in Hampstead, the ambulance crew was amazing, they were so comforting, I remember saying, "Nan keep me, keep a watch over me nan." She was my angel, she was my life, and she would protect me. That comforting feeling would have made me feel better, knowing I was going to be okay. Awab was really shocked and not saying a word, nothing at all, not on the ride to the hospital, nothing. It's always about other people's feeling and never my own - I was more thinking how he was feeling when I should have been worrying about myself. Getting to the hospital I was freezing but the paramedics put blankets on me to keep me warm. They pushed me through to a cubicle to get checked over to make sure I was okay. The lights were so bright shining in my eye. I asked, "What is the time?" It was 8pm.

I still had a small bit of belly cramp, not knowing the afterbirth was last to come out. I was thinking I was sore from the traumatic event that had just occurred.

I rested in the cubicle, lying on the bed drained out but feeling relaxed. Awab was just sitting on the chair next to me. As I turned to look at him I saw in a bowl the two unborn sacks I had just pushed out. A nurse just placed it on the table, not covered and in view so I could see. I stared at it in utter shock. I said to Awab, "Look, look what's there."

Awab didn't say a thing. He didn't call a nurse to say get this away from my wife, are you crazy to leave that there, not a thing. I had to say, "Can you please take it away."

It was now 12am. I'd had my bloods done and I didn't need a blood transfusion which was great to hear. I just wanted to sleep but I was covered in blood and all I was hearing was, "There are no beds available."

I was in the cubicle for hours, bright lights shining in my eyes. I wanted a bath and I wanted to sleep but I was just left in the cubicle. Awab was not even helping me, I had to go to the main reception myself to ask questions and I went to the toilet myself. I started to feel a little more energised, so after I asked how long they were going to be I headed to the toilet, as they kept saying not long. Going to the toilet I pulled down my trousers and plonk a big blood clot thing dropped from my vagina. All the blood that stores itself when you're pregnant finally fell out. After that the cramps were gone but I was completely sore all over and badly in my vagina.

I walked back to the cubicle and got back on the bed. I must have dozed off because the next thing I remember is being woken up by a nurse asking to take my bloods. I was so tired and wanted to sleep but the bright lights were shining in my eyes again. I was fed up.

This young black nurse was trying to take my blood. She pushed the needle in and it wasn't the needles of today, it was a big ass needle. Still half asleep I saw her pull the needle out. "I can't find your vein." She tried over and over again.

"What are you doing?"

"I'm trying to find the same hole that I pushed the needle in already."

I couldn't believe what I was hearing as Awab sat there not saying a word. "Just leave it." I started to get angry and fed up. She left the room leaving me with blood trickling down my arm.

"What's the time?" I asked Awab. It was 2am. I had been left in the cubicle with blood all over me from 8pm till 2am, them still claiming they had no bed. That was it. I jumped up. "I want to go home."

"No Miss Newman," a nurse said, "we will have a bed shortly."

"Nope I want to go home. Look, I'm covered in blood." It had started to dry and stick to me, I just wanted this stuff off me and wanted to sleep. "Let me go home."

"Okay Miss Newman, we have to discharge you and we have to say you discharged yourself."

"Do whatever, you're not helping me here, you've just left me for six hours covered in blood in the cubicle, thanks!" I ranted and raved on.

"Give us a minute and I will discharge you." I headed back to the cubicle still very angry but stronger than before and able to walk around. "Miss Newman can you come and sign here please?"

I don't even know what I signed but I signed it quick if it got me out of that place. I signed and left, no looking back.

Awab and me headed to the bus stop, Awab not saying a word. We waited for the N5 from Hampstead Heath. We were waiting for around 20minutes freezing cold. Thinking of it now I was so silly but that's how frustrated and angry I used to get and if you upset me I'd lose it

Cold, wet and covered in blood me and Awab sat at the bus stop. I just couldn't wait to get home. I started to feel weak again but I didn't care, I knew my bed would make me feel better and I would get the rest I needed. The bus arrived about ten minutes after we sat down and the ride home was quick. I got home in no time, pushing my key into the door. I gasped with relief. Slowly making my way upstairs I started to feel drained. Blood was still in my room and all over the duvet. I collapsed onto the bed, Awab taking my clothes off. I really wanted a bath but by now I was so exhausted and couldn't stand back up.

Awab got a flannel and wiped me down. He cleaned the bed the best he could and I went to sleep. That's all I wanted, just to rest. That's all I needed and I was happy. I was finally getting the rest I wanted.

The next morning I was still numb from the night before, and a little weak. I got up and ran myself a bath. Sitting on the edge of the bath I looked at my tights, the stale blood starting to crisp. I looked at my legs from top to bottom as I heard the sound of the bath flowing higher, devastated to be childless. I always wanted to have my children at the age of twenty-three. I thought that was the right time for me and I was twenty-four so I wasn't too far off. I had been so excited to be a mum, why did this happen? Was this payback? Was this my karma? Why? I asked myself as I laid myself down in the warm bubble bath. Placing my head back I was so heartbroken, but I couldn't shed a tear, I was still in shock.

I'd nearly lost my life. That was more shocking to me, the fact that I nearly died and my own mother wouldn't have given a shit if I did. "Why did you put me in this family? Why did you give me these parents?" I mumbled to myself, questioning God as to why he was doing this to me. No answer from him.

I've always spoken to God from a young age and I felt no connection to him but I believed in him. For every question I asked I never got an answer, so I cursed God, yes I did. I was so bitter and angry I cursed my Father. "Fuck you God, why have you done this to me?" I started to cry, putting my hands over my face in disbelief.

A face appeared from behind the door. Awab. "You alright?" It looks like to get a bit of sympathy from someone you need to shed a tear or two.

"I'm fine," I said, brushing his arm away. "I'm okay, it's going to be okay." I couldn't even look at him. He had just sat there while I was poked, prodded and violated and didn't even say a word while the nurses and doctors spread my legs wide open to examine me inside and out. I felt so ashamed, I felt so disgusted. All my respect and my morals had gone, and Awab didn't even hold my hand for comfort through it. That is not a husband, that is not how someone who cares for you acts, that's just madness.

I knew from then I no longer wanted to be in a marriage or even in a relationship with Awab. I had made up my mind I wanted out and I was planning to leave and never come back.

A few days later I called back to the Royal Free for a check up to make sure I was okay. I felt okay but a little run-down and tired, but more mentally. The check was fine and I got the all-clear to go home. I was told no work and to relax.

At that time I was studying to be a nurse and due to me having a miscarriage prior I'd been out of work, then I fell pregnant six months later, and was still off work. I couldn't wait to get back to work to take my mind off things but my GP had signed me off for another six months for recovery.

After a few days of rest I was ready to go out visiting some people. I just went to clear my head. The more I was at home the more I thought of what had happened. So me, Awab and a few people met up and went to Watling Park. We had a few drinks and a bit of smoke. The day was really lovely and we lay on the grass chatting away. A few drinks down, we decided to leave the park and head back to a friend's house. I wasn't really drinking, I was taking it easy, but I started to feel poorly. I just thought it was due to me being run-down still. I didn't stay long at my friend's home and soon headed back home, feeling extra tired but thinking it was down to the two drinks I'd had. I went to bed as soon as I got home, wrapped up and went off to sleep.

The next morning I stood up and was so dizzy I couldn't stand. I lay down quick and started to breathe deeply. The dizziness soon faded away. I didn't think anything of it, I thought it was just a part of what had happened to me with the miscarriage and my body was still in recovery.

A few days later it happened again. I was walking to my local Sainsbury's and I started walking off balance and everything went blurry. I stopped to compose myself but this time the dizziness wasn't going away and the ambulance was called. I ended up at the Royal Free Hospital again, my vision became more blurry and everything seemed more distant, like I was drunk without a drink in my system.

Soon after I was seen by the nurse and then I had to wait for the doctor. Anyone that knows me knows I can't stand hospitals and the quicker I get out the better. My vision came back so I went home without seeing the doctor.

A few days went by and I was okay, no dizziness and no blurred vision. I was healing and feeling much better.

I was sitting in my uncle's garden, chilling while the sun was ablaze with my cold drink and sandwich, relaxing, not worrying about a thing. That day was so peaceful. I was home alone with no one in my head, no one bothering me. I was stress free. Soon after sundown I headed inside for a nice hot bath then I went to bed straight after my bath.

As I was dozing off Awab returned home and came to bed. It was a really relaxed evening.

The next morning I opened my eyes and everything was blurry and I was unable to see. I felt sick and asked Awab if he was there. He seemed so far away. He chuckled, "You blind man?"

"Seriously I can't see, Awab."

"You'll be okay in a minute, just relax."

The more I blinked and closed my eyes the more the blurred vision stayed. I decided to get up. Maybe my vision would clear if I was active. As I stood up I vomited. My head was killing me and I had to lie down quick. Taking a few deep breaths I was worried but maybe this would pass, maybe it would only be for a few days and I would recover. But I was wrong.

Nine years later and I've had wrong diagnoses, rushed into hospital nine times, sent to many different ENT specialists, brain surgeons and ear surgeons, physiotherapy and still no joy with correcting my balance, migraines and vision.

Now I'm doing it all by myself. How I don't know, but the one thing I do know is that God has always been with me.

My vision didn't get better within the week so I made a doctor's appointment. Awab attended with me. My balance and vision were out of control and I was unable to stand up without any assistance. My GP prescribed me medication for balance and said I'd be okay within a few days' time.

Housebound, I was unable to go anywhere and that was so frustrating for me. I'm an energetic girl and I like to keep active, so I was pretty pissed off when I had to stay home in the hot house all by myself, no visitors and no friends checking if I was okay, no family to see if I was okay. I just lay there rotting away, in bed all day.

The evening came and Awab had made plans to go out partying with his friends. I was so unwell at that time and couldn't see clearly out of my eyes so I needed assistance to get around, and my uncle had gone off for the weekend so it was me and Awab alone in the house. My mother never checked on me so I would be left alone. "Please don't leave me," I begged. I thought something bad was going to happen.

"I'm going out, you're not spoiling my fun," he shouted at me.

I lay in bed thinking, what the fuck did I get myself involved in? I felt trapped. Now I really needed him and he had shat on me. His true colours appeared when I was helpless, now I knew what I was really dealing with: a fucking monster. Unable to retaliate I stayed silent as he left the house to party, not even leaving me a drink in case I got thirsty. How could he do such a thing? How inconsiderate. After everything I'd done for him, this was how he repaid me. I couldn't believe someone could be so wicked but yet again the man who I thought was an angel had turned into the devil.

Unable to sleep for the night I lay alone in the bed, watching all kinds of rubbish. At that time of the morning it was cops and robbers. Even with my blurred vision watching the TV was my comfort. Left alone for the night I contemplated what I had done to my life.

The next day Awab arrived home late afternoon. I'd stayed upstairs just waiting in case I fell down the stairs. Looking all happy he looked at me. "Alright?"

I just thought to myself, wow that's who you really are, and you have a daughter. I knew he wouldn't like a man to do that to his daughter so why did he feel it was okay to do it to me?

Then it clicked. Even though I lived with my uncles they never really got involved in my personal life, I had no father and my mother, well. He knew I had no one really apart from my uncle Keith but he lived miles away. Whenever Keith would call he would go silent, making sure he listened to what my uncle said to me. Keith would always ask if I was okay and if not he would be on the first coach down to Hendon. I never wanted my uncle to fight for me or get into problems for me but just knowing he was there 100% made me feel a whole lot better.

I was fucked. Awab knew I needed him now more than anything and he would use this to his advantage to mentally abuse me at the most vulnerable time of my life. Life became so hard and when you have nothing to live for you just want to end it all.

Life became so frustrating and difficult. I had hospital appointments every week, blood tests every week, MRI scans every other month, meeting consultants, meeting all kinds of medical professionals. I didn't know whether I was coming or going.

The council finally offered me a one bedroom accommodation on medical grounds close to my uncle and mother's home. I lived right in-between them. The flat was unfurnished but I knew I could make it a home. It was the first place that was mine but I was so poorly I was unable to enjoy it. But I just wanted my space for once, a place I could call my own home and this was it. It was my home and no one could control, lie or tell me how to live my life. I moved in in August 2009, four months after I became unwell. I resided there until September 2015. I had some good times living in Marriotts Close, and some horrible times, but I had a home and that made me happy.

I was left in the flat on many occasions by myself while Awab partied and I stayed home feeling unwell. I had no visits from so-called friends as they partied while I was stuck in the house. 2009/2010 had some great summers with parties in the park for the West Hendon community and I couldn't attend any of them. I asked Awab would he take me away just for me to get away from it all. Nowhere special, even down to Brighton would have been nice, but he refused and went out with his friends leaving me home alone. I asked him to start driving to ease the pressure off me going out and walking but he refused. I was so pissed off. How could this man who I married and gave up my life for be treating me in such a barbaric way?

I maintained that when I got back on my feet I was going to leave him and he would suffer because he leaned on me for everything. I was his safety net and he had me where he wanted me; at home sick so I could not meet anyone or see anyone so they could take my attention away from him.

When I was poorly and house bound I never received any visitors the people who claimed to be my friends were partying and enjoying their lives, whilst I sat at home reflecting on who really was there for me. The main person who really took the piss was my mother she would dump my Brother on to me knowing I was so unwell, so she could help her so called friends who would never in a million years help her or watch my Brother. The frustration was real for me and I felt helpless. I was very disappointed in myself for allowing this to happen and I was irritated by the way my mother had been treating me. I love my brother Benji very much and looking after my brother is not the problem, but my mother used me whilst I was stuck at home and she helped everybody else and left me to rot.

The main one was my mum; it was like history repeating itself all over again. The only thing was I was older and very poorly. You really see people's true agendas when you're unwell, broke or homeless. I have seen people's true characters and no matter what they portray to people and themselves I have seen their dark side. They didn't fool me so when they went through problems I just thought to myself, isn't karma a bitch. I guess everyone is due their karma, even me. If you dish out goodness you'll receive goodness and if you dish out badness you will receive badness, it's the circle of life.

I had follow-up hospital appointments, and they found a cyst in my pituitary gland and I was kind of relieved, thinking yes, this is what is causing my symptoms and I will soon be fit and well. It had been long enough.

Mr Neil Dorward, an amazing neurology surgeon, met with me and he spoke to me in regards to my surgery. It was brain surgery but they were going to go through my nose. I was okay with that, in fact I was excited because I believed this was going to get me better and I couldn't wait, risks and all, for it to be over with.

My date was set and I was ready to go. A few family members came over the night before and my mother cooked lamb shank. (Something I now can't stand to eat ever since I was pregnant with Kayleigh. Even the name would upset me.)

I called the day before my surgery 'the last supper'. You just don't know what tomorrow may bring. We ate, they wished me well and I got ready for the next day ahead for my surgery.

On my way to the Royal Free Hospital for my surgery, Awab by my side, the nerves started to kick in. I was a bit anxious but they were happy nerves. Making my way to the ward felt like the longest walk ever and when I got to the ward felt like I was staying forever. My bag, my clothes, my washing stuff; I had my own little quarters.

It was early, 6am. I had to be prepped for surgery. I sat on the bed while Awab unpacked my stuff. Mr Dorward arrived. "You okay?"

"Yes."

"You nervous?"

"Yes," I replied.

"Don't be. Surgery will take thirty minutes if there's no complications and you will be back on the ward shortly after." He explained how he was going to drain the cyst.

"Okay," I said.

"I will see you shortly," he replied and headed off.

A little while later a nurse came to take my blood pressure and give me a gown and some long green socks. "You will be going soon my love, get yourself ready."

I smiled and I asked Awab to help me get dressed. It was kind of weird. If I asked Awab to help me if I was unable to dress or cook for myself he would, but help me get better? That was a no no. I just didn't get it at that time. I had no one else apart from him and I think he contributed to my illness by not helping me when I needed him the most. Awab was very helpful washing me, feeding me, changing me, helping me stand, but that was it. He never helped anywhere else.

THE LOVE OF A MOTHER

It was time. I got called by a nurse and a porter escorted me up to surgery with Awab following behind. Wheeling up to theatre I was starting to get really nervous and now the fear of death did cross my mind. I was only twenty-four years of age and I had lived my life terribly. I made myself a promise if I made it out of this I was changing my whole life completely: the people around me, the man I date, everything, even family.

I got to the door of the theatre and Awab was not allowed beyond that point. Sometimes I do think why did he come? I know he was living with me and I was his main support but he didn't give two shits before. Maybe he thought if he didn't support me and I made it through I wouldn't support him anymore? I don't know but I did find his behaviour so bizarre and strange.

At the entrance doors, ready for my surgery, I looked up at Awab as the tears started to flow. He said bye to me as the nurses and porter comforted me. "It's going to be okay," they said. I always thought I was a tough cookie but even the toughest people have weak hearts.

Going through the doors felt like I was entering the gates of heaven, but the only thing the other side was a cold theatre room. I asked so many questions, that's how I am. I was nervous that if anything happened to me no one would be there to help me, just these strangers who didn't know me at all.

The nurse began to talk to me, asking all kind of questions. I started to feel like I was fading away and trying keep awake, trying to speak. I don't know when I passed out but I know I was feeling very sleepy, and then I was soon knocked out. I was told my surgery took an hour and was very easy to drain the fluid and remove the cyst from my pituitary gland.

Waking up in recovery I was so relieved to be alive. My anxiety had kicked in immensely and I never knew I suffered with it until my surgery. I think because I was unable to see clearly and the feelings I had made me have anxiety.

I woke up in a room blurry-eyed. I saw faintly in the distance a nurse walking away from me. I started to come round and the nurse saw I was awake and came to my aid. "Do you feel sick Katrina?" she asked. I shook my head, still blurry-eyed, still dizzy, and before I knew it vomit came flying out of my mouth. The nurse rushed to my aid with a sick bucket. I continued to be sick; the anesthetic can make you feel this way.

After all the vomiting had finished I lay back down relaxing, tired from the surgery, still blurry-eyed but thinking and feeling this is it, this is what's going to make me feel better and I will be back to normal, back on my feet in a few months.

After an hour in recovery I was sent to the ward to rest. No one was there to greet me. As usual I was all alone.

A few hours later my mum, Awab and my brother Ben arrived. To be honest it was nice seeing my brother but I really would have rather seen a priest than Awab and my mum. It was like they were forced to come up so I had better appreciate them coming. I never liked them doing things for me because to me it was never genuine, there was always a motive behind their help.

Getting the rest I needed I was happy to be in hospital with a little bit of freedom. I was wishing and praying I would get better as soon as possible. I couldn't stay in West Hendon any longer. I was ready to start a new life single and free.

I have to thank Granddad Remy, he came to see me every day in hospital. Remy was in his late 70s but he took the train and brought me a hot chocolate every day. Remy was my neighbour when I resided at Marriotts Close. We became very close and built a wonderful relationship. He looked out for me and I looked out for him. I'm like the granddaughter he never had as he keeps calling me, "Yes my daughter." I will look out for that man until my dying day, he deserves it.

Awab came up every day and I have to give him credit, he washed me from the top of my head to the soles of my feet every day after work. He would bring me food and would stay until midnight, then go to work the next morning. My mum passed up but they were the only visitors to bring me some food.

I stayed in hospital for a week. Hospital gives you so much to think about life, family, friends, and relationships. I was very adamant that when I was better I was off and no return. New phone number, start a fresh life, start my own family, get some new friends, in a new place where no one knew me.

Returning home I was still unable to see clearly and was completely off balance. I needed aid to walk. The doctor gave me the all-clear and stated within due time my balance would be restored and I would be living a happy, free life. Hearing those words 'a happy, free life', with the plans I had, I didn't even mind going home off balance if I was going to be back to my normal self. I was happy and looking forward to an eventful future.

A few days passed and I was still off balance, still unable to see clearly. This turned into weeks and months. I contacted Mr Neil Dorward in regards to my feelings and no improvement in my health. He continued to state "Give it time," but months is a long time to wait to see no improvement at all. My happiness turned into fear and disappointment, upset and anger. I was so pissed off. "Why am I not recovering? Why am I going through these things?" I know people that do terrible things but never go through what I was going through. I questioned, why me?

Back for my routine check-up all my bloods were okay, blood pressure was perfect, my heart was on point, but I was feeling so unwell. Dizzy, blurred vision and off balance, and I was left to sit in a hot flat all day. No one ever even offered to take me out for walks or take me out the flat to get fresh air. I had to try and manage my life myself, and I did. I managed to master where the kettle was, slowly doing little things, but it took me months to do this. I'm an independent person so I would rather try and do it myself. "Fuck them," I said. "You think you're going to have a hold over me? If it takes ten or twenty years I will get better and back on my feet. I will learn the basics of life and start all again."

People laughed when I was learning how to shop or was learning how to cook. I was mocked. "Look, there she goes to Sainsbury's, that's all she knows," my so-called husband, mother and friends would laugh at me.

I never said a word, I just listened. Enjoy your time, God has a better plan for me and I know it's a good one. I had to go through this to make me stronger and stronger, which it has done. I would sit and look at them and think, watch this space, you will remember me from a distance, and one day they will.

As I learnt to get back on my feet again, they watched me grow and when they were watching me grow they started to become nice, but the damage had been done.

It took two more surgeries, physiotherapy after being poked, prodded and operated on. I went private after not being satisfied with still being unwell. What they were giving to me and doing to me was not working. I found an ENT specialist in 2015 in Harley Street and was immediately seen within a day. He asked about my history and examined me. Within ten minutes I was diagnosed with an inner ear bacterial infection with vestibular balance disorder.

Okay, so I'd finally found what I had. Due to not getting antibiotics from the Royal Free Hospital I'd caught an infection that travelled to my inner ear and caused all kinds of madness. Because I was not correctly diagnosed and treated the infection settled and here we are. I suffered for many years for something that could have been treated with antibiotics. Isn't life a bitch? This is why have trust issues - even the doctors are not to be trusted. How can you make such an error at the expense of someone's life?

Now I had the medication I needed to get me better and was going to get fit and well, well that's what I thought. I left Harley Street feeling better than ever and relieved at having a proper diagnosis. I headed home with my tablets ready to take for the week and ready to start to feel normal again.

I don't like taking tablets as it is but whatever was in them was serious. I was getting suicidal thoughts, I was up all night, wasn't able to sleep with bad insomnia, but my vision started to become clearer. I could see! I shouted, "Yes!" This was it. This was my time. I was going to get well.

But little did I know it was the beginning of my journey. Two years on and I'm still unwell but not as bad as I used to be. I see a future and it is looking like a happy one. Finally the tablets cleared up my blurred vision but my balance problems still remain. I'm hopeful for the future, very optimistic, and ready to take the next step into the unknown. I'm getting the right treatment I need under ENT specialists who are helping me the best they can to get my balance correct again.

Throughout my ordeal I was angry and upset with the world and everyone around me. Why did I make that stupid decision of coming back to West Hendon? Why didn't I leave when I had the chance and I had many chances? My uncle asked me to go and live with him when he moved to Manchester. I refused but I should have gone. I had my first place in Camden Town which I left behind for a man, yes a man, how stupid of me. And I didn't take up my uncle's offer because of a man. I'm telling you, I've had many opportunities and blew them and for what? A man, something I would never do before so why was Awab so special or getting the special treatment? I don't even know why myself. Maybe Awab can tell you, but I can't.

I knew what I wanted but still felt kind of lost, like a piece of me was missing.

Soon after my treatment for my balance disorder I was still housebound. I struggled daily. I'm a free-spirited person so someone or something holding me down will irritate me or anger me to the point I will disappear. On many occasions my uncle Keith got that crying call, "I'm coming up NOW!" I would scream down the phone while Keith would reassure me it would be okay. Because I was so unwell I wasn't able to make that move. My uncle was ready to welcome me with open arms. But behind closed doors, brainwashing me, mentally abusing me, was Awab. The saddest thing about my marriage is that I did it to be a wife and a mother, but Awab got married to help him with his status. I was warned by his own friends but I still didn't listen. Awab was a different kind of brother and I had never crossed paths with someone so deadly.

A year into seeing Awab we got talking about our lives and upbringings and I felt comfortable expressing my feelings to this man who showed me he cared. I was genuine but Awab wasn't, he was fishing for information. Awab could see I came from a toxic upbringing with a mother not looking after me and an absent father. Awab knew I was very close to my uncle Keith in Manchester so he would play psychology, he would be the nice man when Keith was around then horrible when were together or around his friends and Family, trying to humiliate me and mock me. But I still stood by him, I guess he played on my vulnerability and I let him. I told Awab of my life experiences and he used this to his advantage to lure me into his trap. He thought I had no one and even tried to turn my own family against me, sneaking behind my back talking about me and talking about our relationship. But little did he know I was being informed the whole time. All the signs were there, I should have run when I had the chance but like I said, I don't even know why I was with him.

Two years after my miscarriage, housebound and with full-on hospital appointments, I fell pregnant. I was so frightened and really wasn't ready to have this baby. I was ready to be a mum but due to being unwell it wouldn't be right for the baby. I knew who I was dealing with and he had shown me a side I did not like. If I needed him I knew in my heart of hearts he was not going to be there for me. So I terminated the baby and cried for days on end. I had made a promise to myself I would never do that again but I did. I was devastated and was so angry that I'd put myself in that situation. I needed to find a way to get myself better as soon as possible.

Awab attended the termination with me. I had an early morning appointment at Marie Care abortion clinic in Warren Street. We got the train from Hendon straight there and it was just a short walk from the Warren Street tube station.

On arrival at the clinic, outside were protesters holding up placards 'say no to abortion', 'you're a killer'.

"Fucking hell," I said, "they're winding me up." Full of emotions I started to cry. I really didn't want to do it but I was so unwell and Awab was not looking after me; the baby had no chance. I quickly ran inside, bowing down my head in shame, pressing the buzzer to enter, feeling even worse. I could see in the waiting room so many women, so many young girls that were there for the same reason as me. Wow, I thought. And this happens on a daily basis, it's very sad.

THE LOVE OF A MOTHER

I stated my name at reception so quietly because I didn't want people to know who I was or even recognize me at all.

"Go upstairs and see the nurse please."

"Okay." We headed to the first floor where the nurse was. The room was very quiet and airy, only one or two women in there. As soon as I arrived the nurse called, "Katrina." I told Awab to stay outside; I wanted to do this alone. "You okay?" the nurse asked. The familiar setting was all that was running through my mind. Here we go again. I knew the routine and was echo hearing what she was saying to me.

After my check over I had a scan and was good to go downstairs to collect my tablets and go home. But once I had taken the second tablet I needed the cab to be there pretty sharp, the miscarrying would happen very soon and I did not want this to happen in the street or in the taxi cab, so I called for a cab just before I took the tablet and headed off home.

I could feel the cramping fifteen minutes into my taxi ride. I was at Edgware Road, a few miles away from my home and when that miscarriage is coming it's not something you can hold in. I managed to get home without bleeding in the car. Awab assisted me up the ramps to my home and I busted straight into the toilet in excruciating pain and cramping. As soon as I pulled down my knickers blood came pouring out. As I groaned in agony I cleaned myself up, taking deep breaths while Awab fixed himself something to eat. I was wishing he would ask me "are you okay" "do you need help" but he just left me there to deal with it.

I staggered to the bed and took the painkillers they'd given me at the hospital. I don't think anyone could bear that kind of pain. I took deep breaths, rocking from side to side as I waited for the pain to ease off. From the corner of my left eye I could see a figure standing at my bedroom door. It was Awab. "I'm going to Edgware to sort out my sound system. I'll see you later." In too much pain to answer I lay there rocking back and forth, still moaning in pain, and off he went leaving me in pain to deal with this by myself. I was unable to stand up; I couldn't even get myself water.

As I lay in bed I thought to my self what a fool I had been. I had made the biggest mistake of my life and it nearly cost me my life. How could someone be so heartless yet want to have a family with me? That's not normal. I knew then I didn't have one piece of feeling for this man. I needed him while I was unwell but as soon as I become well again I'd be off. I would never acknowledge him again.

That day my heart was broken. I had never had that feeling of heartbreak but there and then I felt so unloved. I felt completely destroyed, I was broken into so many pieces it was going to take a miracle to piece me back together again.

There was only one year I can say I was happy with Awab and that was early on in our relationship when we were raving, going to family parties, going to dinner and the cinema, but after that year it felt like hell on earth.

Awab does have a good side to him but I have hardly seen it. I mean if I needed to go to a hospital appointment he would come with me, or if I needed assistance with Kayleigh he would help, but it came with moaning and not really wanting to do it.

He must have something nice about him because I stayed with him for a long time but right about now I can't see it.

I believe he has potential. He works hard but he can't see his potential and wants everyone else to pay for his sorrowful life because he went through hardship.

My motto to that which I have told Awab on many occasions is "I'm not your mother, I owe you nothing so let me be." That has been screamed, shouted and punched out so many times but has never penetrated to get through to him. Awab believes someone owes him something and I believe it must be his mum but I have paid the big price for whatever hurt he has inside of him. Awab had a similar upbringing but without the abuse. He takes all his pain and suffering out on everyone else and if you don't comply with how he feels, well, you don't want to see that side to him, it's like Jekyll and Hyde, it's like someone else comes through and takes him over and there's no stopping him. He will destroy anyone and anything that crosses his path and if you challenge him or have an opinion you will get the full brunt of it. His attitude and stance is intimidating and scary. The mental abuse is overpowering. I've had it all my life so to come from a toxic upbringing into a toxic marriage makes me feel worse than ever.

When I decided to take my wedding vows, I took them very seriously and thought I would at least have a half decent life, not perfect but perfect to me. My children running around, my four bed house with a massive garden and my husband mowing the lawn on the weekend while the sun blazes through the sky and I lie on the sun lounger sipping my champagne listening to Whitney Houston in the background. Yes, I did plan my life out and I knew exactly how I wanted it. But unknown to me the plans for my future were bleak and I faced a big trial and error. I don't know how I made a terrible mistake like that and put myself through that.

I'm now at a time in my life where I just want peace and quiet, no drama, no headache. If I see it occurring with anyone I will distance myself.

I became very bitter angry and heartless. Our arguments were becoming way out of control and I felt powerless because of the situation I was in. I was ill and needed him and he knew this. When I was independent he could not talk to me or deal with me how he wanted because I would not allow it, but now he had the upper hand and I disliked him even more.

There were so many arguments between us one of us could have got injured; it was physical but more verbal. I would cuss him out and he would insult me, that's just how it was, but there were a few things that stuck with me and he really meant those words he would shout out without a flinch or a sorry. If you could have seen his face saying it, well if looks could kill I would have been dead and buried already.

Soon after my termination and miscarriage Awab was being really horrible, and I was getting frustrated by his mood swings and vocal name calling and reminding me of how worthless I was and everyone else was better than me. I would lash out in anger and be very vocal. "Go back to your stinking country go on, get on your banana boat to your hungry family," was one of the famous lines I would shout out regularly.

But Awab's lines were really hurtful too. I'm not saying mine were not but he was not joking, he was not saying it as an argument, he meant what he was saying and he said it with venom in his mouth, his eyes wide with aggression. "You're nothing but a walking cemetery, you're nothing but a whore, no one wants you and will never want you, look at you." My jaw swung open. I never believed he could say something so hurtful and feel it was okay, like it was something normal. It was so disrespectful, I never saw him the same again. How can you look at your wife and call her a walking cemetery and then say you love your wife in the same breath? Awab has said some vile things to me but out of all the words he has expressed under anger that has stuck in my mind to this day. With everything we had been through I didn't expect that. Now I knew how he really felt and he was only with me for convenience.

We both insulted one another but what you say under anger can really hurt people, that's why I say make sure anger doesn't get the better of you. Your true feelings can sometimes penetrate through and sorry might not cut it.

I started being bad-minded towards everyone and anybody who would piss me off, even children got it as well. I just did not care. You could say I had a mini breakdown but it was more me being tired of this life and treatment I was receiving. It was constant, it was like when will it stop? It felt like it was constant since my grandparents had passed away and I was exhausted mentally and physically. I could not take anymore and if I could have run away I would have run away there and then.

I take that experience close to my heart. I always state to Awab what if a woman was just like you? Could you handle it? What if the tables were turned around? Would you stay? Stop and think about it. God gave you two beautiful daughters, what if a man treated your daughters this way? I know for sure he would not want that for his daughters, so why did Awab feel it was okay to treat me in such a way? "I'm sorry" was his favourite phrase but his actions spoke differently. Sorry does not cut it for me. What people say and do under anger, sometimes sorry does not cut it, and in my circumstances sorry was not cutting it for me. Sorry seems to be a sorry word and I was sick of hearing that word. He became a broken record with the extras that he would change and do better. He was just pacifying me so he could continue with his foolish ways. This is where I know lust and love were confused but I'm no longer foolish or confused, I'm stronger than ever.

I should have broken the chains I was in and walked away before it became too late. Love should never hurt.

Awab believes I'm the same person he married in 2007 but that person died inside a long time ago. This is the new me, he won't be able to understand or relate to me. I've outgrown him and outgrown the old me, anyone that believes they knew me won't know me anymore. Katrina Cassandra Newman has been reborn. Far too many people are looking for the right person instead of being the right person.

I nearly lost my life. I took so many things for granted: my life, men, jobs. I have realised that life is what you make it. No matter how or what you feel, I have changed into a better and brighter person. I owe all my glory to God. Without his love and support I would not be here today. He never left me when I failed him and I'm ever so grateful.

Through all the roughness I was still living my best life

CHAPTER 15
FRIENDSHIP

My good friend Stewy, me old china Stewart Sheridan, God bless you, I dedicate this part just for you. Not many people know that you are one of my closest friends and I value your friendship very much. I've known you for over two decades and your friendship has remained the same. Even when I was being a total cow but it wasn't you that was the problem, it was me. I should have been a better friend. I may not see you often but when we do see one another it could be twenty years later and we will still have a laugh just the way we did when we were youngsters running around the West Hendon estate playing tim tam tommy run outs and hunt the cunt. The memories of us roaming around North West London being kicked out of our mums' homes in the pouring rain, walking for hours to your grandparents' home; those memories I will keep for a lifetime in my heart. They are good memories, happy memories. I also know those memories you hold tight in your heart as well. When no one's around we reminisce about our school times and random mad moments and have a good old laugh about it. The only thing we didn't do was go on holiday together, which we should have done but it's never too late. One day we will make that trip and have a good old time like the olden days.

I remember the friendship necklace you bought for me for my fifteenth birthday and my mum got jealous and threw it away. If she hadn't done that I would have kept that for the rest of my life but hey, life goes on. We're older, wiser, and a little smarter with a bit of sexiness. But in our soulful hearts we're Westenders and that stays with us for life. I'm glad I met you, grew with you and have an amazing friendship with you. I will keep you and our friendship in my heart forever.

Love from Katrina.

CHAPTER 16
WHAT ARE YOU RUNNING FROM?

You can never run away from yourself no matter how hard you try, there is always something or someone dragging you back, or God is calling you. Once you are called by the Father you might as well stick your hands up and surrender. I've always been a runner, any problem run from it. I kind of got fed up of the running and faced my dues, dealing with them head on in full force. If you are distracting me I will remove myself, it's as simple as that. If it no longer grows me, supports, encourages, blossoms my empire there will be no need for it in my life, family or not. I finally know who I am and I'm ready for the world.

CHAPTER 17
WHO AM I ? KATRINA CASSANDRA NEWMAN

If people really want to get to know me just ask me, I'm the only person that can tell you about me.

Do your parents even know who you are? Ask them the question, how many GCSEs do I have? Well you can ask my mother and I bet you a few bob she doesn't know how many GCSEs I've got. She doesn't have a clue. She will forever be misled by me because she tried to program me like her and that will never happen because I'm me.

I've always been a private person but people feel it's okay to question and invade my privacy. This is why I distance myself or I clam up or I just ignore them. They're nosy and it's not because they're concerned, it's to be nosy.

I can't remember everything in sequence regarding my life, it would have been easier if I wrote notes down but being so young what was I going to say: I want to die? Because that's how I felt most of the time. I felt tired of life, drained, always wondering when will it end, but just imagine the chance that the pain and suffering your enduring is not down to you, out of the darkness and into the light. When you feel your life is going before you, there is comfort in the new surroundings of a new life arriving.

All I have ever asked for out of life is to be loved, what was so hard in doing that?

I always felt and feel I'm the black sheep of the family. Being seen and not heard, I felt a loss of my power, my mindset, my strength, and now I was ready to take it back.

It was when I first looked at the scan I knew for sure this one was going to be special. Kayleigh–Jade Jah Princess Felix, what an outstanding name. The meaning behind Kayleigh's name is 'undefeated', how special is that? Yes I picked a good 'un.

Before I knew I was pregnant, I remember I could not stop being sick, up down, up down, to the point I was so tired of being sick. I was telling myself no more sick, closing all the curtains to block the rays of the sun, opening all the windows for fresh air, smelling the green grass that had just been cut by the local council. I lay on the sofa holding my head. Why was I feeling so ill? What had I been eating? I remembered a few days prior me, Lisa and Awab had eaten a kebab and I was adamant I had food poisoning. I kept asking them were they feeling sick.

"Nah," they replied, "I'm alright."

For fuck's sake why was I so unwell? All I could do was drink water and sleep the day away. I had given up the thought of being a mother due to my balance and vision problems. So when I was still feeling unwell I headed to my local walk-in centre to get a check over just to make sure I didn't have food poisoning. When the nurse explained to me I was pregnant I could not believe it. I was being very careful because of me feeling so poorly but clearly I wasn't being that careful; all it took was one shot.

Finding out I was pregnant was scary but a little exciting. I was going to have a child. I begged Awab, "Please I will need your help." With all the lies he had told me throughout the years I had no choice but to trust him. I went straight home and back to bed.

The next morning I was feeling very tired but still excited. I was going to be a first-time mum, I was adamant I was going to have a boy but finding out I was having a girl I was a little upset. When the nurse told me, "Katrina I don't see a little winky," I already had a name, Shermar, and stuck with that name until I started buying baby girl clothes.

My pregnancy was traumatic and tiring. I was in and out of hospital, vomiting, you name it I went through it. I was fed up of being pregnant, it wasn't a nice experience being pregnant but it was nice carrying a beautiful baby, and she was my baby. April 9th 2012 Kayleigh-Jade Jah Princess Felix was born at the Royal Free Hospital, seven pounds exactly.

When Kayleigh was born it was like a breath of fresh air. The birth went smoothly, it was a natural birth and I didn't need any stitches and I was able to walk out of the ward, something they had never seen before. Once Kayleigh was born she was stunning and so quiet. I kept looking at her, smiling. Awab was staring and smiling at her. I didn't know what he was thinking but he looked happy. I was overjoyed but drained out to the max; all that pain and pushing had tired me out.

Kayleigh was here and I knew, ill or no ill, I had to step up my game and now be responsible for another human being. I knew it was going to be hard but I was willing to do this. I was passionate about being a mother and I was ready to step up. I kissed Kayleigh on her forehead and gently whispered in her ear, "I love you Kayleigh and I will take care of you for the rest of my life. You have nothing to worry about." I knew my life had changed forever and it made me happy.

Kayleigh is now six years of age and is one smart, beautiful little girl. She makes me laugh and sometimes cry. She vexes me sometimes but I still love her the same way. Kayleigh has changed my world for the better. She has taught me what unconditional love is. My heart is open so that I'm able to love others. I crave a love so deep and can't wait to find the love of my life, a man who will love me and Kayleigh without limits and we will love him the same. Awab will always be a part of Kayleigh's life and everything we've been through has made us become good friends. With all the trials and tribulations we made it out as good friends for the sake of our child and I'm happy with that. I hope Awab finds the love of his life and lives happily.

I don't like to blow my own trumpet but I will, I deserve it. I'm a star in the making and I know my potential. I know what I can achieve. I'm ready for life and there is nothing that can stop me. I'm fully focused. I'm kind, loving and have been always loyal with a slash of a bad ass temper that I'm trying to control through counselling and controlling how I respond to situations. Not everything needs an answer or a response but I need to know how to handle it. It was hard to begin with but I have learned to tolerate people that like to hear their own voices.

I love who I am now and I know when people are taking the piss and when I feel that kind of energy I distance myself

My clock is ticking; I'm thirty-four years of age and want to live the rest of my life happy with loads of enjoyment. I feel I've missed out on so much when I see people all loved up cuddling kissing laughing and you can see genuinely that they are happy and in love. I really wish that was me, I need love to carry me high. I don't think anyone can love me the way I need to be loved. I have high expectations when it comes to love, I want it in abundance. If I fail at life, if I succeed, I would have lived as I believe. Learning to love yourself is the best love of all. The remarkable thing about my life is that I'm writing about it today after overcoming fear and the battle within myself. Isn't that ironic? Isn't that amazing? I think it's bloody brilliant. A young lady with a dream who thought her dream was only a dream, but inside of that there was a young star born with a story to tell the world. As a grown woman she took the challenge and made it visible, making it her duty to share her story. Change is good and in order to change you must be vocal to express your untold emotions. The definition hell on earth for me is not the person I want to be, I had to transform my vision. Finding my true identity was very important for me in order to present myself in the correct manner because I'm an influence for so many people, the main person being my daughter Kayleigh-Jade. I need to show my daughter that anything in life is possible, and that you shouldn't let fear conquer your heart. Everything in life is achievable and through me my daughter shall learn from my corrections.

The power of negativity is listening to people that tap into your inner emotions, who end up making you talk to yourself or questioning yourself out of something that could be the biggest change of your life.

The power of positivity (Look from Within). The skills and love that have been given to you can only shine out, lifting your hands up embracing the beauty from inside of you. The feelings that you had stuck inside will start to make you understand how you're true feelings are supposed to feel. When you start to feel the reality of the love from within you will start to cry, not because of sorrow but because of the joy and happiness that is starting to flow and then you will start to let go and let love in.

'GOD IS WITHIN HER, SHE WILL NOT FAIL.'
~ PSALM 46:5

CHAPTER 18
TRUST

Imagine having to doubt yourself or something or someone you thought was unquestionable. Imagine having to question the one person who is supposed to protect to you, losing all trust and never being able to trust again. There are two things in life I don't trust, I don't trust men and I don't trust people.

I've been let down too many times by people close to me and I have been destroyed by men. When you've been hurt so many times you become numb. You feel numb and if something bad occurs you don't even flinch, it becomes so normal.

For me to let a person in I will have to feel they're different and even then I will still feel they have a hidden agenda. I will never believe a person is hundred percent pure-hearted and that's sad because I know there are good people out there in the world, I just got lumbered with the shit people.

I believe trust is earned and when you have earned your trust nothing else is questionable. Once trust is broken it can never be repaired. Trust takes years to build but can be destroyed in a second. Forgiving someone isn't the hard part it's all about trusting him or her again, and if they continue to break that trust it's best to leave that person alone. Don't ever be sorry you trusted a person, that's their problem not yours.

The best proof of love is trust. When you feel free to trust someone the love for that person becomes unconditional. Once you love without restrictions and love without fear respect is due from there. Trust goes a long way. It's something people take for granted, but not me. When I lose all trust in you, you will have lost me and all my respect and it will never return. I will be nice and civil but my loyalty will never remain the same.

Trust is about listening without interrupting, speaking without accusing, giving without sparring, praying without ceasing, answering without arguing, sharing without pretending, promising without forgetting, forgiving without punishing and loving with an open heart

I don't want to change a thing about the people I've trusted because trust revealed their true characters to me, but I would have changed the way I trusted them. We live, we love, and we learn, and I have learned so much from so little.

Trust can be a bitch but can be so beautiful. Trust your instinct, it will never lie to you or let you down. What you feel and what you see is the reality of people. Never let the judgment of people confuse your inner feelings.

CHAPTER 19
DEPRESSION

This major word, depression, is controlling mankind and people's lives. Well not mine. When I was sixteen years of age my GP diagnosed me with depression due to the impact my lifestyle had on my life and me.

I was feeling very low and wanted to leave this world so I made an appointment to see my GP about the feelings I was feeling. My GP listened and examined me and thought the answer to my feelings was for me to take anti-depressants and gave me a pill to take. She said, "Take it and it will make you feel better." Take this? I thought. Are you mad? This is not going to make me feel better; this is going to make me feel worse. I know what is making me feel sad, I know what is making me upset and it's not depression and these pills are not going to help me.

When I hear the word depression I feel it's a trapped word that society wants to make you feel.

Do you know how much those pills cost? They cost a fair bit of money and the pharmaceutical business is a big one. If most of the country or the world was all under pressure to be depressed you have just made the government very rich.

Take a holiday, hit the gym, spend quality time with your loved ones, spend time with friends, talk about your feelings, Nothing is impossible and your life will start to unfold. Your life will start to reveal itself, your life will start to blossom and you will start to feel happy. Change your mindset ...

I'm not taking depression lightly, I believe depression is a very serious illness and I know people suffer with depression really bad. Some people's mental health is out of control and they really need to take anti-depressants and really need help. But for my situation I didn't need the pills, I needed a genuine helping hand to get me out of the rut I was in. Until this day aged thirty-four I have never touched a single antidepressant. I believe in self healing and as hard as it can be it works for me. I observe what is causing me the pain and heartache, I address it and deal with it the best way I can. I always remind myself life is really worth living.

CHAPTER 20
PERFECT LOVE

The power of love! That's all I need right now, my main desire. Overwhelming love, passionate love, giving love, the love that just flows and you know it's true. The love that you just know you are loved. My next spouse will have to understand that I'm in it for the long run and there are no games to be played, but this time round I know my Lord will send me the correct man. I'm more than ready for love. If only I controlled who I was before, humbled myself and listened. It's all about discipline of the mind. I'm going to face the unknown but the unknown can only be great. I'm open to it. What is love? I believe love is a soulful feeling, a feeling so strong when two people are joined together. There are no limits on how they love one another, they feel so open and free. Love is honesty and trust. Without these two in a relationship love will not come through. If you ever plan on loving somebody make sure it's the right love, love can be so precious and so kind. Love is not just about relationships it's also about friendship. When you find a soulful friend who you connect with and share special memories with it's a one of a kind love, a love you can't buy, a love you can't force. It comes naturally with the twinkle of an eye with a personality to match. If you have this you are gifted.

Everything I've been thrown my whole life the Lord knows it hasn't been pretty but I just knew that there is prettiness out there.

I'm looking for that needle in the haystack that fire they can't be outed, someone so different that when I see him his eyes start to shine & glisen Penetrating through to his soul that feeling when you know you found the one.

CHAPTER 21
MY FATHER

How can I explain myself to the Lord? How can I express myself to the Lord? The one thing I do know is when the Lord is calling you, you might as well stick your hands up and surrender. You can't fight the almighty force of the Lord's spirit and when the Lord's spirit touches your soul, you will know about it instantly.

My Father touched me in the one place I never wanted to open: my heart.

Before I was saved, I wasn't a bad person I was just bad to myself and did a few wrong things. I had no self-love, no self-care, feeling in such a way made me feel confused and lost. I was lost to who I was as a person. Coming from such a toxic upbringing can really distract you from yourself. I was floating around trying to find my way in life, until one day, and I remember it like it was yesterday.

I was hosting that Christmas. My family came over and we were playing music, dancing, drinking, and having a good time with a good Christmas dinner. Something drew me to look out of my living room window and there was a shining star above my home. It caught my attention and I wondered why that star was placed above my home. I had all kinds of feelings but the one feeling I felt was peace, like nothing and no one could trouble me.

Months later I had forgotten about the shining star above my home. I was going through some serious trials and tribulations trying to fight them all by myself. All of a sudden I got that feeling again of inner peace, like everything was going to be okay. For once in my life I listened to the inner feeling and I finally knew my Father was calling me. I surrendered and gave everything to my Father.

I can't go into details but what I can say is I'm here today with a different mindset, a different way of thinking. I'm at peace. God opened doors, closed doors, and now I understand why. Not all negative situations are negative; they can be blessings in disguise.

I owe everything to the Lord, the good the bad and the ugly. With all things that have occurred in my life it has made me the person I am today and I'm ever so grateful.

My Father was there to catch me when I was falling and He raised me up. At this present time I'm healing my mind, body and soul and with my healing I'm able to heal others. This is why I call myself God's Gift. Many people including myself have been through heartbreak but maintained. I call these kinds of people God's gift.

My Father, my main man, my keeper, oh how I love you so much. You have been so good to me, you are a glorious God, you are a forgiving God and you never gave up on me. My Father does not hide in the shadows. His presence is vibrant, energetic and loving. He loved me when I failed Him and showed me the way.

If you want to make this world a better place start from within yourself and the rest shall fall into place. I will honour, serve and adore my Father until the end of time. He is my life.

CHAPTER 22
I NEEDED YOU

All you need is love and the people that care about you. Love can be a terrible feeling when you love someone and you can't have him or her to love, all because you didn't see it at the time, or due to circumstances, or you messed up your chance. It can make you feel so low and so unwanted. I can never forget those words 'I needed you'. Maybe I needed you too, I'm sorry you needed me and I wasn't there for you,

I believe in love at first sight and I believe in soul love. People fall in love in the most particular ways looking into each other's eyes or just spending quality time together.

I can't believe the person whom I would claim as a friend is my soulmate. How? I have never felt this feeling before, is it real? Is it facts over feelings or is it just a phase I'm going through? I have questioned myself a million times, why him? Something I would never do is asking someone else's opinion about a guy because I've never been in love or felt the need to question my feelings before.

This time I did not care; I was losing sleep over someone I didn't even see or speak to regularly, but I do know what I was feeling was coming from my heart.

I look back on the day he asked me to be with him; maybe I should have jumped at the chance. Maybe he did need me but I was as lost as him. I know he's upset with me for this but everyone makes mistakes, just like he has and I never judged him for his but he has judged me for mine. This breaks my heart. I wish he got to know me, the real me, the gentle, caring, loving with a fiery temper me. Yep, that's me. I know what I want and I know what we both deserve and that is each other, I can feel it.

Robbed of our happiness, we left it too late. I know we will never be together and that's such a shame. He has so much to give; he has a beautiful heart with an uncontrolled temper. He needs to heal his heart so he can have a loving future. I believe you were sent from Heaven. I was saving all my love for you, why didn't you stay? #MYSOULMATE

CHAPTER 23
I CRY

Have you ever cried invisible tears? Tears from your heart? My tears have always been invisible. I keep all my pain inside and smile through all the bullshit, holding my heart while the tears flow from within.

One of the things I love because it always intrigues me is personality and I'm going to tell you why.

I keep a lot held back, but many people can express their emotions and feelings in different manners or ways. I've seen people physically broken or mentally broken. I have seen people broken but unable to show emotion but their eyes tell you a thousand stories. These are the people that really grip me, maybe they remind me of me. You will never know what they're going through or what they're thinking but you just know that person is going through something so agonising. You can see the tears in their eyes but not one teardrop comes through. Their personality remains the same, caring and loving. A person's characteristics form their qualities as individuals observing and identifying.

So when a person can identify their pain and knows how to mask it, their facial expressions, their personality and their character will tell you a completely different story to what their eyes will show you.

My tears will forever be invisible because that's how I deal with pain, that's how I mask it. Cry from the inside and hold your head up high and just keep moving. My confidence has been flattened. I was afraid to show who I was, battered and bruised. It is now time for me to be the person I want to be. When you start to feel unliked and your personality is shoved aside you start to feel irrelevant and overlooked. I'm the only person who can change how I feel. I'm the only person who can open the door to my heart.

CHAPTER 24
SANDRA NEWMAN

My mother Ms Sandra Newman was born on 6th April 1966 at West Hampstead Hospital in North London.

My mother has eight siblings including one older brother in St Kitts. One brother passed away in 2012, my uncle John, due to liver failure. He became dependent on drink when his parents passed away, something he just could not handle until his dying day. May he rest in eternal peace. The rest of her the siblings are living their lives.

My mother attended Hyde Primary School with her other siblings and went to Hendon High School with her sister Shirley while the others attended White Fields.

My mother and her brothers and sisters had a tough upbringing. My grandfather was an alcoholic. He was violent towards his wife and children, something I never saw growing up but I'm fully aware of it from the constant stories I hear playing in my ears like a broken record playing over and over again. When you hear of a sad story long enough you start to think to yourself why don't you just make a song about it since you love it so much. It's crazy how people's minds work and can't let go of a history or an event that is no good for their mind, body or soul.

My grandparents were good to me. My uncles and aunties tell me stories of how bad my grandfather was which is sad but to be honest that is not my problem, I can't take someone else's pain away, he was not bad to me. I can sympathise with how they were treated but my grandparents are dead and buried over two decades and are not here to tell their side of the story.

My granddad's violence had a massive impact on all of their lives and a lot of them are in denial in regards to the way that they feel, how life goes on.

How I see it is your sin is not greater than another man's sin. A sin is sin. We all sin and if you have sinned you expect to be forgiven for your sins, so why can't you forgive everybody else? We don't know people's hearts. But I do understand each sin has a greater consequence than others.

I love my uncle Keith's attitude. He moved away and started a fresh life, a happy life. He told me one day when I went to visit him, "He's not here anymore. He done what he done but I have a life to live so I'm living it." And believe me my uncle is living his best life.

My mother on the other hand is not living her best life. She is living a sad life at home drinking, smoking, not doing anything with her life. My mother had many good jobs growing up but her last job was at the DWP office but due to her circumstances she gave up her job in 2003 and has not worked since.

My mother is a very intelligent woman but can also be a manipulator. If you don't know her she can convince you that you are mad and make you believe it. That's how deadly she is. I always state that a person making themselves knowledgeable through reading books isn't necessarily knowledgeable. A person can educate themselves beyond belief and still be unknowledgeable? Because they don't use their knowledge wisely a person with knowledge might not even know how to put a lightbulb in because they feel they have knowledge, but don't have any common sense.

Some people use their knowledge for power or to belittle people. Do you know the most educated people are wise people with no knowledge? A person with no knowledge will master the gift or craft God has given to them with confidence and pride and will educate people along their journey.

I will take any day a person unknowledgeable over a person with too much knowledge, they appreciate life and our souls.

I stress this to my mother regularly but whether she takes heed of what I state is up to her. With all the knowledge she has she can put it to good use. My mother is very generous and very helpful towards others. She will go out of her way to make sure someone in need or someone

THE LOVE OF A MOTHER

who is elderly is well looked after. She's helpful and has an open hand. She is funny as well, something I learned after spending the past year getting to know her, it's something I have never done before.

My mother has spoken to me about being raised in a toxic household. It is very daunting and I will never understand what she faced growing up but I do know I felt some of what she faced because of the way she treated me.

My mother is the full-time carer for my brother Benji who will soon become an adult and I wonder what she will do when he no longer needs her assistance. Will she ever work again? Will she ever live a happy life? Throughout my life my mother has drunk, smoked and taken drugs. It is a part of her lifestyle and I believe she enjoys it very much. She likes living that oii oii let's 'av it kind of living.

When my mother was thirteen years of age she was run over coming home from Hendon School while walking with her older sister Shirley. She has a massive scar on her left cheek but if she doesn't tell you about her accident you wouldn't know that the scar was there.

It was a serious accident and she nearly died. She was run over and dragged down the road. She was in a coma for months and had to learn to walk again. She had a massive head injury which could have affected her personality and way of living. She received no care, no love, no attention and her father tormented her after she was run over, telling her to cross by the lights next time.

She was locked away for over two years and when she fully recovered she rebelled and lived a crazy life of drugs, sex and alcohol.

All the anger I had for my mother for the mental abuse, I never knew half of the stuff that happened to her growing up and I still don't know the full impact of what she faced. She talks to me about things but she does not go into depth about her struggles and problems. As I've grown I have come to an understanding it wasn't an easy ride for my mother but I still did not deserve that abuse from her. I have realised she was struggling with life and when her mother passed away her main rock was gone and she thought her life was gone too. Even though my grandmother had nine kids and an abusive husband she kept the family educated, they had morals, were respectful and she kept them well fed in the hardest times in Great Britain in the 1970s when you cooked your food from scratch.

It took me over thirty years to understand and forgive my mother. I can see that's all she knew and she continued the cycle. She has told me many times that it was never my fault that she treated me that way, but as a young child being constantly told you are worthless is very hurtful and heart-breaking to hear from your mother. She says it was her that was destroying me and I knew this but for some things it's too late to turn back, the damage has been done. But you can fix it and make a positive situation out of a negative.

I'm cool with my mother and have no malice towards her. I still don't accept and like her ways but I have come to an understanding that this is her character and she will never change and that's okay, as long as she's not damaging people along her journey. People are changing and people want a happy life, not a life to continue from something that has no value or is time consuming. If you dwell on the past negatively you will forever live in the past and your life will be full of negativity. You can talk about your life experiences not in a manner to make it control your journey or experiences. The past is the past, you cannot change it but you can change how you live your present. You are in control of your destiny.

This is a message to my mother: pain changes people. You are rich in love. Find what you love and go live it. I hope life treats you kind.

THE LOVE OF A MOTHER

Me & my Mother at her 50th Birthday Party, we had a Blast that night good times good energy with good people.

My Mother on the West Hendon estate in the 1980s

CHAPTER 25
FORGIVING LOVE

Let us start to forgive each other, only then will you find inner peace. When you're weak-hearted you can never forgive. Forgiveness starts with first asking God to forgive you for your sins, then asking God to forgive those who have sinned against you.

When you forgive you heal and when you let go you grow. There is no man or woman on this earth who is not sinful. Show me a person who isn't. If you want to be forgiven for your sins you must forgive others. Do not hold that burden in your heart; it is too much to carry.

I was able to heal my heart by asking God for his mercy, for I had forsaken him and shown him no love.

I asked God to share and shine his grace upon me for I feel lost without him. I asked God to show me how to love myself, show me how to forgive, show me how to love others.

God answered my prayers and let love into my heart. Once I was healing I asked God can you heal my mother's heart and show her how to love herself.

No matter what people have done to me I will never have hate in my heart, I only want love inside of my heart and that's how I'm going to keep it, my love is internal. There is nobility in compassion and empathy in forgiveness. It shows maturity. Your character really defines you, this is why I state be careful what you say and do to people. Sometimes sorry does not cut it.

I believe forgiveness is a purpose of life and you must forgive to set yourself free. A person does not need to be in your life to forgive them.

Make peace with the Lord, make peace with yourself and let go.

I have learned that people will forget what you said, people will forget what you did but people will never forget how you made them feel. If you're sincerely and genuinely sorry I can forgive you in a heartbeat. Forgiveness is not the problem, it's the mockery behind the forgiveness.

Family is very important to me so it's very easy for me to forgive them. Family is one of life's greatest blessings, a unit of people that love and support one another and once families understand the meaning of family then all shall fall into place.

I'm asking God to please forgive me for messing up the blessings he gave to me. I see everything clearer now and I pray he shares his grace with me.

It feels like I just walked right out of Heaven. Forgiveness and love always win in the end.

Kayleigh and me spending quality time together, mummy loves you very much always and forever

THE LOVE OF A MOTHER

Me and my beautiful brother Benji

Benji and Kayleigh

KATRINA CASANDRA NEWMAN

Every *picture* has
a *story* to tell

THE LOVE OF A MOTHER

Me in happier times

KATRINA CASANDRA NEWMAN

I'm thankful for everything I have

CHAPTER 26
POURING OUT MY LOVE LETTER

I have read so many books that have given me amazing knowledge and mental understanding, they explain all about good Women, good Men, good relationships and a good marriage. What Men need to know about women and what Women need to know about Men is when the opposite sex are combined together they become one. It is committed energy, time understanding and knowing each other's qualities. Men are leaders, lovers, guides, and protectors. The lord made men and women so unique, he made a man so powerful and women to help grow a foundation and bring forth life. The creation of the world is so unnoticed the information of finding the perfect partner comes from wisdom, information, knowledge, and strength the more you know about your partner the more you study your partner the better your relationship shall be.

Let me start with humbling my beginnings. I have asked the Messiah to make me a great Woman before you make me a wife. Make me ready to be a lover, make me ready to be with knowledge, make me ready to be my husband's peace make me ready to uplift my husband to his best ability. To be ready to set a foundation and stand firm when my husband needs me to be ready to be a Mother to be ready to be a wife. I want to be ready for my husband so I can show him that his future image is a great one and I believe in him. I want a man that walks with the Messiah not perfect but a man that knows his purpose and knows where he's going, a man that will protect my solid ground and will protect our relationship because I will love him rich or poor, it's his heart that I want and only his heart I will keep.

The Man Messiah has for me is family orientated, free-spirited, he knows what he wants he is a leader and is ready to grow as a unit my perfect man needs to tick 3 boxes! I'll keep the 3 boxes to myself but what I can say when my King comes to connect with me I'll be ready and I know he would have been sent from the Messiah

   I love, love and love, loves me

CHAPTER 27
THE OLD DEAL

On reading my book whoever you are and whatever back ground you come from I hope you learn a great deal from this book. I want to hear from you and learn from you, I'm still on my journey and I never stop learning. The preconditioned me with the old mind-set I've pushed aside because I see a better and beautiful me. It shows that dealing with obstacles can have its benefits including its flaws, but in all fairness the reality of the obstacles has made me realise what I have been facing.

THE NEW DEAL

What can you call a new deal? What can you call a new life? What can you call a new year? What can you call a new you? What can you call a better you?

Well let me make this clear, it's very simple. The deal is YOU. That's it you! Your happiness is you the new deal you are looking for is you. You have to remind yourself that you are the only person that knows what you want out of the life you want to live. There can only be better from bitterness, so take the new deal and make a better YOU.

CHAPTER 28
THE FUTURE AND GIVING BACK

I don't know what the future has in store for me but I do know I can never make those kinds of mistakes again. That was my past and this is my present, I'm very excited for the future, I know it's going to be a happy one. My life has turned a major corner and there is no turning back. It had to start with forgiveness and I started with forgiveness in me, and then I could forgive others. What you see is what you get. I'm ready to be there for others, people that really need me and I will not let them down. God opened up the door for me, door after door after door keeps on opening and I'm thankful. My life is not perfect ands I'm not as healthy as I should be but that is not stopping me from achieving my dreams. At this present time I'm working on getting my health in order, focusing on my daughter's future goals and accomplishments. In July 2017 I started fulfilling the start of my dreams. I successfully finished the Inspiring Women business program. All 23 women passed. We made the national paper as the first group to ever accomplish this achievement together. This is one of my biggest achievements so far. In August 2018 I was awarded by the Mayor of Barnet two awards for my support within the community. Stepping forward, stepping up and stepping out for giving my generous gift of time, I was very happy.

My life is taking a better turn for the future. I don't think people have ever seen me smile so much and talk so much of happiness and love.

I will work with children who have autism and ADHD. I feel this is where I'm needed; this is where my heart is. I have an insight into children who suffer with this and they need my help, starting with my brother Benji.

Whatever blessings come my way I will not shun in vain. I will be open and embrace it with open arms, smiling, and enjoying the ride.

THE LOVE OF A MOTHER

I'm starting to build an amazing family unit with my daughter and me. I look forward to an outstanding career and of course there are going to be ups and down but I know how to handle them now and treat the down days as a good day, ignore it and be patient.

I have given my life to God, one of the best things I have ever done in my whole entire life, and once you do that your whole life changes. You will see the real people come to light, the real people who love you, the real people who support you and the real people who will care for you. I love myself beyond measure, and I love every minute of it. I feel I've taken so much from God, used and forgot about him. There is no way I can pay God back but the plan is to show him that I understand and I'm here to serve him.

Sometimes we get a wake-up call, and I'm grateful I did. Some people don't get a second chance at life but God has seen my heart and knew my heart was tender. All he had to do was open it.

It's my time to give back to my Father, the community, my family, friends and most of all, my daughter Kayleigh-Jade. I'm far from perfect and I'm going to make mistakes, I'm human, but as long as my heart is pure and in the right place and I know where I'm going everything will be alright.

In my new chapter I would like to give back. It's something I feel I need to do, and I'm guessing it's God's plan. I'm the CEO of God's Gift, which I set up in April 2014.

The inspiration behind the name God's Gift comes from the many women including myself who have been through hardship, struggle, pain and suffering. Some women have overcome their struggles, some women have overcome their pain, some women are still going through their life struggles but throughout their pain and suffering they still maintained a pure, good and beautiful heart.

These women are trying to find their way in life, trying to find happiness, trying to find love. I call these women God's Gift. Many women have come to speak with me and have opened up about their life struggles. I don't know why, maybe they trust me, maybe it's God. I listen and take in and feel everything they're saying. When you can relate in some way it's easier to listen and understand their pain. My loyalties are always with the women who feel they can trust me.

I will be running a workshop called Gods Gift. It will be a charity based workshop to help vulnerable women back into society with life skills, a place where they can come and relax, talk and find peace with changing their lifestyle in the process.

I'm a small pin in a big wheel but I'm here to make a difference. Even if it's a small difference it's something, but I'm not here to make a small difference, I'm here to make a big difference, impacting and encouraging women into a bigger and brighter future.

Helping people really makes me happy. Seeing a person happy and smiling, knowing I have made a difference in that person's life for a split second or a lifetime is the best feeling ever.

Writing my autobiography was very draining and it has brought up things I'd left dead and buried. I never want to relive those moments again. I want my life to be filled with positivity, happiness, travelling the world and lots of enjoyment, focusing on Kayleigh-Jade's future and if I have more children, their future. I never want to look back in the past and if I do it's to look back on how to better myself.

I know my upbringing has had a massive impact on my mental health and well-being and how I used to treat men and people. I try my best to overcome this by thinking positively. I put all my energy into seeing the goodness in all situations, good or bad, and that works for me. I always state you can turn a negative situation into a positive and I'm the prime example of that.

The relationships I have with my mother and Awab are building slowly. We have started to see how we are as people. We communicate more, trying to rebuild a relationship we never had. They are set in their ways and I accept this. How they want to live their lives is up to them, but I can only be civil. We've come on a long path and it was very hard for me to accept but we passed the worst.

For the sake of my daughter I will try my best to co-parent and have a good relationship with Awab. No matter the circumstances between Awab and I, my daughter's best interests are my main concern.

In 2017 I reconciled my relationship with my biological father Ronald Thomas. It took the death of my uncle Little Man AKA Sydney Huggings who is an uncle to Ronald, so out of respect I have to call him uncle. Uncle Little Man died from cancer at the age of 83 in 2017. He desperately wanted Ronald and I to have a father-daughter relationship and he got his wish just before he passed away. It took over two decades for me to even accept him in my life, but I believe people deserve a second chance so let's see how it goes. Kayleigh-Jade adores her grandfather very much. It will never be how I grew with my grandfather but at least he is trying to make amends and make an effort.

My mother, well, my mum is my mother. She has been chosen to be my mother and I don't question it. I can only keep my mother in my heart and hope she finds her way. I will be amicable and understanding as much as I can be. I felt like I was never good enough for my mum and that's sad but I will still keep guiding her forward. Our relationship has become better than it was. We will never have that mother-daughter relationship, it is too late and that is very sad.

But we can only try to continue to build on this one day we will be in a much better place with each other.

ACKNOWLEDGEMENTS

I would like to first of all thank my Father the Lord, my God. Without his love and guidance I would not be writing my life story. He has helped me turn all my feelings of pain into a beautiful blessing, keeping me strong and grounded, guiding me and keeping me on the right path.

I would like to thank my uncle Keith for always being there for me no matter what I do. You also look out for me and correct me when I need correcting. You teach me so much about life and make sure I'm always safe. You deserve the world.

I would also like to thank Caz Kennedy, my mentor, for making me understand who I was again and also for making me remember nothing is impossible.

I would also like to thank Amanda Blossom who inspired me to start writing my autobiography

I would also like to thank the people who have been a part of my journey.

I would like to thank my family who are a big part of my life, may God bless you all.

Thank you to Awab, you have had a massive impact on my life; the good, the bad and the ugly. Thank you for giving me Kayleigh-Jade, our beautiful blessing from God. May you open your heart one day and find the love you're looking for. Our journey was a harsh lesson in reality and has made us grow in so many ways. I ask God to heal your wounds and guide you on a magical journey for the rest of your living days.

I want to thank Kayleigh-Jade. I love you ever so much and I'm grateful you are a part of my life. Thank you for being you.

Mummy loves you.

I would like to thank my brother Benji who I adore. You have a wonderful outlook on life and I see how you must feel in your little bubble. You're an awesome young man and you have many things to offer the world. Take every opportunity to live it to the fullest. You are God's gift.

I would like to give my thankful and final acknowledgement to my mother, Ms Sandra Newman. I thank you for giving me life. Your lessons and blessing, your lifestyle and our journey has made me the person I am today. You can always turn a negative situation into a positive.

I wish you all the best in life and I forgive you because I understand that your upbringing had a massive impact on your life journey. It is very sad that you never got to feel the love you should have to make you grow into the beautiful woman that you are. May you find inner peace within your heart so you can heal and live a happy and eventful life, just the way you wanted to. I love you Mum. Love from your daughter.

ABOUT THE AUTHOR

Born and bred in London England in 1983 Katrina Cassandra Newman grew up in North West London, on the West Hendon estate and now lives in Mill Hill, North London. She is an up and coming film director and is also a mentor for vulnerable women running a workshop called God's Gift

Katrina states

"The one thing I know is people are going to judge you regardless. Let them. Everybody has a story. There was an untold story inside of me and it caused me much agony. My life story might encourage others to speak out about their life struggles. I have empathy for those who have had a tough ride. It's not just about the trials and tribulations but the goodness of life, inspiring people to love themselves, the reality of who we are and what our purpose is."

Life changes, I feel different within myself. The way I dress, the way I talk, the way I present myself is ever so different. I'm not going backwards anymore. This book is my closure to my past for me to move on towards my future. Sometimes you have to look back just to see how far you've come but that's as far as it goes.

Milton Keynes UK
Ingram Content Group UK Ltd.
UKHW021949211223
434647UK00002B/3